A LIFE WELL WORN

A COLLECTION OF PERSONAL STORIES

A LIFE WELL WORN

A COLLECTION OF PERSONAL STORIES

LARRY SCHREIBER, M.D.

The following pieces were previously published in literary journals, sometimes in different forms:

Anak Sastra
I Know Your Heart

blood and thunder: Musings On The Art Of Medicine
The "Good Doctor"
Doctor and Father

Breath And Shadow
The Other Side

Dirty Chai
Sometimes It's Just A Smile

Eastern Iowa Review
Khmer Rouge Welcoming

**Lime Hawk Literary Arts Collective –
Parts Unbound, A Mental Health Anthology**
Psych Ward 1973

Manifest West, A Literary Anthology – Western Weird
Joe Shorty's Curse

Neurology
The Dance

Twisted Vine Literary Arts Journal
Mr. Jablonski

War, Literature & The Arts
Nong Chan Camp—Rice In Her Mouth

I would like to acknowledge the following people:

Veronica Golos, my editor and literary guru, who pushed and
prodded and spent hundreds of hours with me and who put up
with my computer illiteracy and believed in my story;
without her it would not have been told...

David Perez, my co-conspirator, with an eye for the
heart of a manuscript...

John Nichols for his long-standing friendship and good heart...

Cover photo by Lenny Foster
Author photo by Jim O'Donnell
Designed by Lesley Cox, FEEL Design Associates
Copy editing by Donald Baucom, Monica Wesolowska, Barbara Scott,
and Pamela Giannatsis

NIGHTHAWK PRESS
TAOS, NEW MEXICO

Nighthawk Press LLC, P.O. Box 1222, Taos, New Mexico 87571

To my wife Catherine Strisik—my poet, my grounding point in this world, who never lets me get by with excuses for anything. It is her heart which nurtures me and chastises me (all in a good way). She lives for writing, and it is her fervor that allowed me to venture out.

Zanzibar, 2011

Dedication

To my children, who make it all worthwhile, albeit a little too exciting: Matthew, Michael, Jordan, Mary, Champa, Lucas, Kevin, Gina, Gabrielle, YoRi, Lorena, Ciela, Reynaldo, and Dimitra.

In memory of Kevin
September 3, 1975 — May 22, 2010

Table of Contents

Foreword

met Larry Schreiber close to 40 years ago, shortly after I moved to Taos in 1969. He must've become my primary care physician a few years later, meaning that for the past four decades we've had a close friendship that includes hiking together to the top of relatively big mountains near Taos; Larry checking my prostate gland annually; many dinners and events at his San Cristobal home surrounded by his confusing hordes of children; and moaning and groaning to each other when times were difficult for both of us. I even served for a few years on the board of Child-Rite, a private adoption agency for special needs kids that Larry ran for years.

On several occasions he quite literally saved my life, most spectacularly by diagnosing a rare endocarditis infection inside my heart, which came within an inch of killing me at age 53. Instead, Larry's intuition and his expertise added—so far—another 22 years to my life. I am now 75, and every morning I wake up I thank my lucky stars. I also thank Larry Schreiber. So how could I not praise this book?

Being a great doctor, however, doesn't guarantee that the doctor can write. Larry has always been able to talk, schmooze, tell a story, be humorous, be serious, jabber on in New York slang, laugh at the foibles of humankind. He is articulate, funny, real smart, involved with the world, a born storyteller, charismatic, and adored by the people he serves. We have exchanged both hilarious and serious conversations all the years we've known each other. We can chatter.

But then, get this: a few years ago Larry tells me he's going to write a book. Really? Immediately, I wonder: How can this mensch, this bon vivant, this father of 14 children, this compassionate doctor who treats every patient like his personal best friend (and means it), this director of the Child-Rite adoption agency and the Taos hospice program, this person who seems to be on call 48 hours a day and who has literally *no free time ever*—how can this charismatic sawbones who is now, in his mid 60s, also dealing with Parkinson's disease … how can he ever find the time, let alone the skill, to write a book?

Timidly, a couple of years ago, Larry gave me a folder with four or five essays in it. I chopped them to pieces, suggesting that he needed to learn grammar, punctuation, sentence structure, descriptive writing, pacing, word choice, you name it. I am not a vicious critic, but I try to be honest.

Months later Larry gave me another folder of essays to read. I read them and thought, Oh my gosh, *these essays are getting a lot better*. The man is *serious*. He is learning the craft at a remarkable rate.

Swish-pan to an evening at the Living Light Gallery in Taos not long ago, where Larry gave his first public reading. His off-the-cuff verbal introduction to his essays was wonderful. Larry is an effervescent and raconteur; he can move you to tears and laughter in the same breath. But what comes across immediately, once he begins to read his first essay, is that this successful doctor is not only an extremely likeable human being, but he's also a writer. A real one.

How did that happen? It should be against the law. I myself started writing when I was 11 years old. It took me eight lousy (unpublished) novels and hundreds of lame (unpublished) short stories, and myriad stupid college newspaper humor columns—plus a lifetime of reading novels and nonfiction books—to finally produce a semi-decent manuscript that actually got me published.

Larry Schreiber, on the other hand, sits down at age 65, starts recording his fascinating memories, and Presto! His stories, adventures, heartbreaks, and joyful times are spellbinding, entertaining, rigorously memorable. He's not only a natural-born storyteller, but a natural-born writer as well.

I think this book is beautiful. The life it covers is truly 'well worn' and also one lived to the hilt. Sometimes the essays deal with tragedy—yet they are also filled with joy, humor, and the awe of being alive. They are enriched by Larry's commitment to healing, to unselfishness, to embracing without fear the complexity of existence, and always with the humor that is at the heart of his survival, of *our* survival as a species.

And, especially, these stories are filled with love.

The essays are remarkably clear, simple, and unassuming. They are moving, gentle, lively, and shining with a depth of compassion not often expressed in such a relaxed and simultaneously profound manner. Every page seems to be imbued with wonder, with fun, with poignancy. Larry tells about his wayward childhood back East on Long Island; his first clumsy attempts at becoming a healer; his crazy decision to attend the anti-diversity military college, The Citadel, and how he managed to escape by the skin of his teeth. We are privy to the hellacious vagaries of medical school. And then treated to the lunacies of being an inexperienced and destitute doctor, in destitute Northern New Mexico, involved with overseeing a wayward psych ward, the Indian Health Service, and the sometimes 'life-threatening' Questa clinic, half an hour north of Taos. People die in his arms. Doctors can't always save the patients they care for most.

Larry Schreiber's life story is a love poem to Northern New Mexico and to all its inhabitants, as well as to Larry's own children—so many of them adopted—and to his wife and friends and colleagues. His travels take us to a Cambodian refugee camp during the horrors of the Khmer Rouge regime. And there is a rich, and I think wondrous, tale about his complicated visit to India to adopt his daughter Gina.

Almost every essay is inspiring, touching, and also gentle even if hilarious. Some experiences bring forth a tear without ever being sentimental. Most of these pages produce a smile. Yet Larry also takes us through his first experience with AIDS in Northern New Mexico; the bitter filing of a malpractice suit; and how it feels when your cherished daughter almost bleeds to death after the birth of her child. Too, there is a moving eulogy to one of his kids who died tragically.

Full disclosure: You know already that Larry is one of my dear friends, and, as my doctor for almost 40 years, I have profound gratitude, affection, and admiration for him. But that is beside the point, I promise.

I've been a professional writer for over 50 years, and I take the craft seriously. And I am moved to say that *A Life Well Worn* is among the most humane and decent books I have read in a long time. It's engaging and generous, and it certainly stole my heart. I consider it a merciful and considerate antidote to many of the stresses of our time while dealing with the stresses of our time.

It's Larry's first book. I hope the first of others to come. My friend has climbed up to 20,000 feet in Nepal, and he actually summited Kilimanjaro in 2011. However, to my way of thinking, this memoir is one of the higher peaks he's climbed. Sure doctoring is difficult, and so is raising 14 children. But becoming a writer into the bargain? That would be like climbing Mt. Everest, backward, in the nude, blindfolded, and without oxygen.

With this book, my pal has done that. Larry's reach has exceeded his grasp ... and that's what a heaven is for.

— JOHN NICHOLS, DECEMBER 2015

John Nichols with Larry in San Cristobal

John Nichols is the author of *Milagro Beanfield War, On Top of Spoon Mountain, Nirvana Blues, Conjugal Bliss, Sterile Cuckoo,* and 15 more books. He lives in an old adobe in his beloved Taos, New Mexico.

The Dance

Seven years ago, on a brisk fall day in 2008, my wife, Cathy and I were hiking on the north ridge above our home in San Cristobal, when she asked me, "How come your right arm isn't swinging?"

"Oh, it's just my rotator cuff."

Now, I'm a good diagnostician. Months later, one afternoon, the muscles of my right hand felt as if they were shaking. I looked down; my hand was still. It was an internal tremor, like before an earthquake. Almost as if my body were reading a medical text, I noticed my fifth finger twitching, and that's when the thought came to me, quickly, then was immediately dismissed.

A few months afterward, I was, well, hard to say this, I was on the toilet. I had developed constipation, which I'd never had before. Still, I wasn't adding up symptoms. As I sat there reading *Sports Illustrated*, my right hand started a classical 'pill-rolling tremor.' I knew right there I was done. I had IT.

I went to Lucas, my son, who is also a doctor, and told him all the signs. It was unfair of me to lay this on his shoulders. Like me, he didn't want to say IT. He wanted his father to have a long, healthy life, which got in the way of his speaking the words neither of us wanted to hear.

Finally, Cathy, Lucas and I went to a movement-disorder neurologist, Dr. Sarah Pirio-Richardson. As we drove from Taos to Albuquerque, we attempted to keep things light and optimistic.

"You just have a twitchy body, Larry," Cathy joked.

"You probably have an atypical essential tremor," Lucas added. "You're getting old, Pop."

We arrived at Dr. Richardson's office, and she invited us in. There were three chairs set out. She watched me walk, moved my arms around checking for rigidity, watched me write, and ten minutes later said: "You have Parkinson's."

Parkinson's. *Paralysis agitans*. I had always liked the contradiction in the name: paralysis and agitation. You can't move when you want to and can't still yourself when it matters. In medical school we would imitate the shuffling Parkinson's gait and festination—the inability to start and, once going, the inability to stop. And now I had IT. I was shocked to my marrow. I had become that caricature, that patient.

On the way back, we were quiet for much of the ride. Lucas drove. Once home, I felt it necessary to immediately call those members of my biological family who could have a predisposition, a genetic link: My brother Ken, my sister Sue, my son Jordan, and my daughters, Gabrielle and Dimitra. I told them each the same thing: "I have early Parkinson's. It's just starting. Don't worry. I don't even need meds yet."

Gabrielle sobbed. Jordan was quiet. Ken was speechless.

Dimitra asked, "Am I going to get it?"

Sue, as always, said, "You'll be alright."

In medicine we say, "Genetics loads the gun; environment pulls the trigger." If you look at the brain, deep in the brain substance lays your basal ganglia. There lives your *substantia nigra*. It's dark black. It's the place where dopamine-producing cells thrive. Dopamine is a neurotransmitter that affects movement, mood, emotions, your sense of self. By the time I began having symptoms, I had lost 70 percent of my dopamine-producing cells. There was no going back.

I had my DNA checked and was relieved to discover I had none of the 'known' genetic aberrations. This meant that my biological children had the same chance of having Parkinson's as the general population. Great news. Yet I had caught it. I logged onto my desktop computer, looking up Parkinson's. Now I was searching as a patient, the doctor in me asking all the questions.

What were the early signals of this disease? Let's see, I lost my sense of smell about 15 years ago. I didn't think much of it then, even as a physician, although I missed the scent of Cathy's skin. Smell is part of the aphrodisiac of loving. Then there's coffee in the morning. The smell of turkey roasting. My grandchildren's sweet smells. I'm a hiker, the smell of the forest.

Were there environmental triggers for me getting Parkinson's? As a child, when I visited my grandparents, who lived in Morris County, New Jersey, trucks loaded with DDT sprayed the Lake Hiawatha neighborhood to kill mosquitoes. Along with my friend Steve, I would run behind the trucks, playing GI Joe, thus inhaling the odorless but deadly pesticide.

In San Cristobal, New Mexico, where I live, I had a 30-year battle with prairie dogs, which were destroying my fields. They carried insects that cause bubonic plague. Imagine. So every summer, I tried to kill the prairie dogs without chemicals. I threw bubble gum down the holes, hoping they'd eat it and get intestinal obstruction and die. I shot them with BB guns. Nothing worked. Then I got the bright idea of using cholinesterase inhibitors, a close relative of nerve gas. I was actually trained by the Department of Agriculture to be an 'official' prairie dog killer, as were all my patients who had to deal with the pesky varmints. Here's how you do it: First you insert a long black plastic tube in the prairie dog hole. Then you carefully take out the aluminum phosphide pellets, force the pellets down the tube, then pour water in the tube to activate the poison. Voilà. So there I was, day in and day out, intent on murdering while using surgical gloves (what was I thinking!?) and a surgical mask over my mouth and nose.

What probably did me in though was the misuse of pesticides during my three months in Cambodia. The British doctor who was responsible for Public Health came to me one day with panic in his voice. This was near the end of my time there.

"I've been spraying the hospital, as you know, Larry," he said. "To keep the flies and mosquitoes off the infants. But I just realized that I was spraying the insecticide undiluted. I think I've made a mistake." The instructions stated that the poison should be diluted 200 to one.

I remarked, "So dilute it!" and went back to work in the chaos of the camp. I wasn't worried about the future then. I was in the moment.

I believe this is the moment that eventually got me.

I've done my bargaining with God. *If I do everything right, will you let it progress slowly? If I continue working, will you slow down my tremors? If I accept my condition, will you help my daughter, Gabrielle, become pregnant? If I love everyone to the best of my ability, will you...*

And now? I exercise, I move, I climb mountains, do tai chi. I even meditate. I try to stay positive and accept what has been dealt to me. And actually, it's been a pretty good hand so far, at least at the time of this writing. Yet sometimes I balance my acceptance with my frustration, and fight. Then I say: "Fuck tai chi, fuck meditation, and fuck you Parkinson's. Do your worst. Try to ravage me. If I live long enough, you and I will fight to the end."

––––––––

If there is one thing I've learned in this crazy and love-filled life, it is that easy is not necessarily better. Raising 14 kids, doctoring in an economically deprived community, starting an adoption agency, and now, coming down with Parkinson's, is hard. But within the difficulty is beauty. The feeling of 'coming through.' As Marian Wright Edelman, founder of the Children's Defense Fund says, "Service is the rent you pay for living."

My wife is a poet and writer and has often remarked that I'm a good storyteller, which is true. Whether it's speaking at conventions or telling stories to my kids, I know how to weave a tale. I enjoy it. But I'm not a writer, which of course didn't stop Cathy from one day saying that I should write a memoir.

"This could be part of your new life," she said. "Oh, the stories you have!"

"That's the problem," I replied. "There are so many! Where would I start?"

"Begin at the beginning, that's always good."

"Which beginning? Becoming a doctor? Becoming a father of 14? Moving here to Taos? Cambodia?"

"I don't know. Take your pick. It will keep you busy, Larry."

Busy. Yes, that's always good.

And so I began to write. And write. As I suspected, I had many stories and many beginnings. The Parkinson's has made it difficult at times, but I plugged away. Much of what I wrote read more like vignettes, while other stories felt more fleshed out. The life I've had!

I'll start at the very beginning.

My Mother's Kitchen, My Father's Shoes

Once a month on a Saturday, my father dyed my mother's hair in our small kitchen sink. Black. Black dye all over the sink, the counters, towels, everything. My mother would scream, "Not that way, Sam!" or "The water's too hot!" They'd giggle like children.

Our kitchen was so tiny we had to fold the Formica table into the wall to walk through the room. Linoleum floor. Metal sink. White cotton curtains on the one window. This was East Meadow, New York. Late '50s. The house had a side door; we could go down to the basement or enter the kitchen. When I was growing up, the basement—a piano, a couch, and a desk—was where we brought our girlfriends.

My mother, Jean, was warm and extroverted, singing throughout our small house. She'd belt out Ethel Merman's "There's No Business Like Show Business" as we got up in the morning. She wasn't a great singer—she'd always been in the chorus—but she was a phenomenal dancer, who performed in vaudeville in Boston and New York. She'd show us photos of her dancing in these different shows, with the group Jean, Flo, and Ann. It was sometimes difficult for me to see the photos, because she was only 'scantily clad.' My mother earned $16 a week, and my father, $12. But when they married in 1937, he insisted she quit dancing. Even though it cut

Larry's parents, Jean and Sam Schreiber

Susan, Larry and Ken

their income in half, he felt too old-fashioned to have his wife dancing in strange cities far from home. I suspect that he also missed her when she was away.

Unlike her dancing, my mother's culinary skills were limited, even challenged. Inside the refrigerator, she kept a jar of schmaltz; pure chicken fat we spread on rye bread—we might as well have injected it directly into our left main coronary artery. But we enjoyed it anyway. On Mondays, my mother always made mishmosh, a 'delicacy' that's hard to describe to anyone else—so tasteless now but so delicious then. To create the mosh, mom mished together ground meatballs, potatoes, ketchup, and Le Sueur peas. We felt special having Le Sueur canned peas, which we thought were almost aristocratic. They had a French name after all. Years later, my brother and sister and I did not understand when our respective spouses refused to mish the mosh, choosing instead to eat the meatballs, potatoes, and peas separately—*and* too politely!

My maternal grandparents came through Ellis Island from Minsk, Russia. They came at different times. His name was Woolf and her name was Miriam. They were renamed by the officials in Ellis Island as William and Mary. They met at a dance in New York, where Willy flirted with Mary's younger sister, who told him, "My older sister, Mary, has to marry before I become involved." So Willy, always the cheerful opportunist, married Mary. He was only 17; Mary was 24.

Grandfather William learned the furrier trade in America. Family legend has it that he "fooled around." When my mother was young, he left. And didn't return for an entire year. When he came back, my grandmother asked, "What happened Willy?"

"I got on the wrong boat," he replied.

They stayed together for another 50 years.

I loved Grandma Mary. We called her 'Little Grandma,' because she stood only four feet eight inches tall. She was a short ball of energy, always talking and laughing—a real pistol. When I was a senior in high school, I had a 1961 Pontiac Catalina. I'd plan a day with Little Grandma, and we'd take a drive through the tonier neighborhoods of the North Shore of Long Island.

"Grandma," I'd say, "Can you believe these houses cost a hundred thousand dollars?"

She'd just shake her head and smile. "Faster, Larala, faster!" She loved speeding.

Our general practitioner prescribed vitamin B12 shots for Little Grandma. He hadn't found a vitamin deficiency. It was a placebo that gave her energy. The GP taught me to give her the shots. Every time I did, she gave me three dollars. So on the weekends, when I wanted to go out, I'd tell her, "You look tired, grandma. I think you need a shot."

"Good, boychick," she'd say.

Seconds after the shot, she'd exclaim, "Larala, I feel better already."

My paternal grandparents, Esther and Hyman, came from Odessa, Russia. His last name was Torah-

Schreiber. Somewhere it's likely that his male ancestors were probably scribes—people who copied the Torah. Be that as it may, the name Torah never made it past Ellis Island.

In 1912, my father, Sam, was born at home on Houston Street on the Lower East Side. His father died in 1918 from the Spanish flu. Esther was alone. Rumor has it that charming Willy, my mother's father, had an affair with Esther!

Big Grandma Esther (in contrast to Little Grandma) towered at five feet one. She had white hair down to her waist, which she wore in braids around her head. She was beautiful, but cold. Her apartment in the Bronx smelled like stale overcooked onions that always put me to sleep immediately. Her apartment overlooked Yankee Stadium, and when Mickey Mantle hit a homerun, the entire apartment shook from the roars and applause.

My Aunt Beatie, my father's sister, lived with Big Grandma and didn't marry until she was 45. The marriage lasted one year. She lamented to my mother, "I feel so bad I lost my virginity to that man."

My mother, in classic form, replied, "What were you going to do Beatie, pickle it?"

Our Great-Grandma Bubbe (on my father's side, Bubbe being the Old World Yiddish term for grandma) was religious. She would fly in from Omaha, Nebraska, for her visits. Being Orthodox, she'd be put on the plane by her daughter, Yetta, but never on a Saturday. My father would pick her up and bring her to our house. When she came to visit, we had to 'play' kosher: Keeping separate dishes for meat and dairy, and throwing out the bacon we all loved. I used to sneak into Bubbe's room to peek

at her shaved head, her sheitel draped over a manne-
quin's head. Some Orthodox Jewish women, when they
marry, shave their hair, and wear a wig.

For the rest of the year, we were more 'modern.' Even so, each Friday, with or without Bubbe, my
mother took out the Shabbat candlesticks. They were
silver, 14 inches high, set together on the table. Friday
nights, she'd cover her eyes with her palms, waving off
the secular world and blessing us all—the matriarchal
world of Judaism.

In 1960, it was time for my bar mitzvah. For religious Jews, no work or travel on a conveyance is permit-
ted on the Sabbath, Saturday. This meant that Bubbe,
who was 98, wouldn't even let my father push her
wheelchair. So we walked. And we walked. Because
Bubbe moved so slowly, it took hours to go half a mile.
I remember walking behind her, she in her black dress,
her legs bowed, in heavy black orthopedic shoes. She
always wore black, as a widow. After my bar mitzvah
at the East Meadow Jewish Center, my father had us
wait with Bubbe until the sun went down. Then the
Sabbath would be over. While we waited, my father
walked back home, got the car, and came to pick us up.

———

My father was good looking, resembling Robert
De Niro in *Godfather II*. In great contrast to my mother,
he was a very quiet man. He worked for 43 years at
Macy's at Herald Square, on 34th Street in Manhattan.
Every morning, 7am, he made himself Maxwell House
Instant Coffee, drank it, smoked a cigarette, drove his

1947 Dodge to the Bellmore Train Station in Long Island, rode the train for an hour, then exited at Penn Station on 34th Street. In Macy's, where he started as a 'stock boy' in 1933, he rose to be an executive. Because of his father Hyman's early death, he'd dropped out of school at 16 and went to work to help support his mother, brother, and sister.

After he married my mother, in order to get work he lied on his application to Macy's, saying he'd attended New York University. Years later, when he was an executive, he taught a weekend course in business administration at Harvard. I overheard him speaking to my mother, saying, "Can you believe it? I was a high-school dropout and now I'm teaching at Harvard." He turned to me, knowing I'd overheard. He looked embarrassed. But I was proud of him.

My father made us all breakfast on the weekends, eggs and bacon. After it was cooked, he'd take the bacon and put it on a brown paper bag on our Formica table, so the fat would drain off into the paper. After my mother died, my siblings and I found love letters that he'd written to her when she was working as a dance counselor in a summer camp in the Catskills. They were full of mushy sentiments: "Oh I love you, I can't wait to hold you in my arms," etc. It almost seemed as if someone else had written them.

In another letter, he wrote: "The loan for the trucking business will probably come through." We never knew he'd applied for a loan, certainly not a million-dollar loan! And he wanted to start a trucking business? I guess they didn't give him the money, because he always worked for Macy's. Nevertheless, my father impressed on us kids that we should work for ourselves.

"It is important to make your own decisions, and not be under a boss," he said.

My father came to my Little League baseball games straight from the Bellmore Railroad Station, still dressed in his suit and tie. He'd sit on the bleachers, away from the other parents, like a dark shadow above the Bermuda-shorts-clad summer folk. They'd all be talking to each other and yelling for their kids, while my dad sat silent, smoking a cigarette, staring at me. I knew he didn't want to be there, but he was a man of duty, and duty was how he showed his love. When I hit my first and only grand-slam homer, he was there.

I will never forget my father's shoes, always shined and ready to go to work, the practical, dependable, obligatory, need-to-must-go-to-work life. I stared at those shoes when he tied my tie, prior to bar mitzvahs, weddings and funerals. He struggled with my tie, as I looked down at his shoes—polished, laced black wingtips—his breath on my head, ashes from his Winston cigarette falling by my face. I told him I could tie it myself. But I hoped he would never stop. For it was there that we lingered together as father and son.

The Jelly and the Hot Dog

The summer I turned 14 I worked at Mr. K's Supermarket, stocking shelves, making a dollar an hour, watching the 1961 wave of Long Island girls shop for their mothers as I fiddled with my apron, bored to tears. Fortunately, my sister, Sue, rescued me from oblivion and drew me into her world at the Cerebral Palsy Center in Roosevelt, Long Island.

"Why work for Mr. K's when you can come to the CP center with me and volunteer?" Sue asked.

"To do what?"

"You could help with the feeding of the kids, among other things."

"Okay."

So that's what I did. I had no altruistic purpose. I was simply curious, and it looked like something that could break the summer monotony.

But before I continue with this part of my story, there is something you should know. I was a neurotic kid. Case in point: I couldn't stand jelly. Hated the smell, texture, and taste of it. The very thought of jelly invading my body repulsed me. This is important because, as it turned out, it was a cerebral palsied boy named Brian Brown who would change the way I faced my life.

Each group of handicapped children was named after East Coast trees; I worked with the 'Elms.' The Elms were kids with average IQs who were afflicted with cerebral palsy and muscular dystrophy. They ranged from fully ambulatory to those with all four limbs affected, to others with athetosis (involuntary movements) caused by RH negative sensitivities. This was in the days before preventive treatments had been developed.

OK, here's where the jelly comes in. For me, what could be more disgusting than eating jelly? Feeding it to drooling CP kids only three years older than me. This was my job at the center. For eight weeks I fed them jelly. Then one day, I realized I loved the kids more than I despised jelly. It was love that became the task, not the jelly. This wasn't an epiphany type of moment, just a slow realization from weeks of looking into the eyes of those kids, recognizing that I was doing the right thing. And isn't that what life should be? It was like I had come home to myself.

When I became a doctor, the mechanics of helping people was full of distasteful acts. It's never pleasant to have an alcoholic vomit on you or doing a sigmoidoscopy—looking up the rear ends of people. But the feeling of helping always overcame my apprehensions. And it all was born at the CP Center feeding the kids jelly.

I worked and played at the Cerebral Palsy Center for seven years, all the way up to the age of 22. I worked every summer and Saturdays during high school and college. I even spent a summer externship with the pediatric neurologist the summer after I finished my first year in medical school. My closest friends wheeled or pushed their way into my heart. There were touch football games where Roger Ghersoe fell or flung himself out of his wheelchair to make the reception. The physical therapists always turned a blind eye to the damage we did to the chairs.

The summer after I graduated from high school, just before going to college, my friends from the Elms planned a surprise going-away party for me at one of their homes. Doug Winterfelt and I went together to Lou Pappalardo's house, which had stairs leading down into the basement where the party was held. When we got inside, I lifted Doug into my arms and carried him downstairs into the basement. When the waiting group yelled, "Surprise!" I dropped him right on his ass.

Then came the summer of 1963, and the fateful Mets baseball game, where I almost killed Brian Brown. We sat in the left-field bleachers, Brian in his wheelchair with his neck awkwardly twisted to the right, watching the Mets lose to the Cardinals. Both of us, adolescents with short attention spans, tried to pass the time without focusing too much on the game as the Mets continued their slide down below 500. I bought a hot dog, a plain ballpark hot dog. Not kosher, not really a New York frank either. Brian smiled. I knew what he wanted, he who had taught me how to feed him jelly without my throwing up. He opened his mouth and from five feet away, I took set shots with pieces of the hot dog. I missed the first four throws, and then swish right into his mouth and directly down into his trachea. I watched, horrified, as Brian turned blue.

"Oh my god, I'm killing him!" I yelled. Then Salvatore Gullo, the physical therapist, sprang into action. In those pre–Heimlich maneuver days, he lifted Brian by his legs out of the wheelchair, hung him upside-down, and pounded on his back until the aspirated piece of hot dog shot out and hit me in the abdomen.

On the way home on the school bus, Brian laughed about this. Many of the kids like Brian, who weren't verbal, had what was called a word board. It had the alphabet and keywords on it like "No" or "I'm hungry." Pointing with his head, Brian told me silently, "I had fun."

I had learned another valuable lesson: Sometimes you have to take risks to lead a fulfilled life.

About Face

My brother Ken was a legend even before he was suspended. He was seven years older than me, and I thought he could do anything, including date Natalie Wood.

"Hey, Larry, I'm gonna date Natalie Wood."

"All right!"

Ken wore cool clothes: Winston cigarettes tucked under the sleeve of his tee shirt. Leather jacket with the fur collar turned up, boots black, Levi's with rolled-up cuffs, tight. An Afro before Afros were fashionable. On senior day, when everybody did silly things, he rode his bike through the halls of our high school, East Meadow High.

My brother hadn't been much of a student, by choice. My parents went to see Mr. Lovejoy of Lovejoy's College Guide, in person, and paid him $50. Lovejoy's recommendation: "Send him to military school."

No problem, thought cool Ken. He ended up at The Citadel, the military college of South Carolina, a college proud that it was so tough it made West Point "look like kindergarten."

While Ken was at The Citadel, I memorized the Plebe Handbook he had given me as a present. I was in middle school and thought the handbook was cool. I still remember parts of it:

"Why do plebes come to the mess hall?"

"Sir. Three times a day and even more often,

lowly plebes come to the mess hall to make sure the upperclassmen are properly served, Sir!"

Call these little ditties cries of manhood or sheer stupidity. Whatever the case, but after high school I decided to follow in Ken's footsteps and enrolled at The Citadel. My friends couldn't believe it.

Steve Horowitz said, "Are you out of your mind? Why the hell would you want to go to a military school?"

"Because it's tough!" I crowed.

"That's not you, Schreiber."

I knew on some level that Steve was right. It seemed so childish to say I looked up to my big brother, Ken. All my friends were going to East Coast coeducational schools, and even before the Vietnam War, military schools were just not on the usual New York radar. My parents were more understanding, although they did say that I shouldn't feel pressured to do what Ken was doing. In the end, they supported my decision.

So it came to pass that in the summer of 1964, I enrolled in Company F at The Citadel. Once there, from the first moment, I hated it. I mean hated it. Our company would assemble in a quadrangle, the surface of which had been painted in a red-and-white checkerboard pattern. Here I would stand braced, with my M1 rifle on my shoulder, while an upperclassman, only 19 years old, screamed in my ear, "You're a piece of shit, Schreiber!" No wonder The Citadel had the highest dropout rate of any freshman class in the country, but one of the lowest after the plebe year.

There were only seven Jews in my freshman class. There were no Black men. No women. Each Sunday we were ordered to pray. Jews pray on Saturday. But on

Ken and Larry

Sundays, we Jews were marched to a small room in an academic building where an upperclassman handed out the siddur, the Jewish prayer book. All told there were about twenty Jews in the institution. The Christian soldiers marched with drumbeat en masse to the chapel.

After three weeks, I was ready to abandon my first try at 'machismo.' Even though I didn't share The Citadel's core values, I wanted an acceptable way of leaving. But how do you do that?

One day, while playing basketball, a classmate ran into the pole that supported the backboard and basket. He broke his nose and was screaming and bleeding. All I could think of was: "What a lucky guy, he gets to go to the hospital."

Soon after that, in the mess hall, the place I hated and feared the most, an upperclassman threw his glass in the air. This meant I had to catch the glass and serve him. He wanted ice in his milk. I caught the glass, put milk and ice in it, and presented to him. He stuck a fork into my wrist and remarked: "It's just like your kind to be cheap on everything, even the ice."

I bled on the table, hoping it wouldn't stop, so I could go to the hospital. No luck.

By this time, my brother was stationed at Ft. Gordon, in Georgia. One evening, I was called to the company commander's office. I saluted the guard who was in the office: "Sir, Cadet Recruit Schreiber, L.H., reporting as ordered, Sir." And from the uniformed officer came a reply: "Asshole, it's me, your brother, Ken."

We hugged. Ken had graduated from law school after The Citadel and was then faced with two choices: Join the Army JAG, which meant three years of service, or to take his military commission and flirt with the possibility of going to Vietnam for 12 months. Ken hated the army so much that he took his chance with the military commission. Luckily, he got to spend his two years in Georgia and New Jersey.

The company commander allowed me to go on leave with Ken for a few hours. Yet all I could think about was Saturday-morning inspection the next day. My brother, always cool, always setting an example, had two motel rooms, and, as was usual in those days, two girls. Anyway, I ended up in the other room, napping. My brother entertained the girls. He also shined my belt buckle and my shoes so I could pass inspection early the next morning.

—————

South Carolina in 1964 was overtly racist and hostile to its Black population. Strom Thurmond was one of South Carolina's senators at this time. He stood in opposition to the Civil Rights Act of 1957. Indeed his filibuster against this act lasted for 24 hours and 18 minutes, the longest ever carried out by a lone senator. He and much of the white population of South Carolina were also against the 1965 act designed to end segregation and protect the constitutional rights of African-Americans—including their right to vote. Thurmond insisted that: "All the laws of Washington and all the bayonets of the Army cannot force the Negro into our homes, into our schools, our churches and our places of recreation and amusement."

The Citadel reflected these sentiments. One afternoon, which was the final straw, an upperclassman told me, "Get me more mashed potatoes."

I held up his plate, a signal for the African American waitress, a matron with an apron and hair covered by a light-blue kerchief, to come over. "Ma'am, can I have more potatoes?"

While she stood there, the upperclassman said, "What did you call her?"

I replied, "I called her Ma'am."

He said, "You call her waitee, or you call her nigger."

Sheepishly, I called her "waitee."

I knew then I had to get away. I regret I did not call him on it.

The next day, I waited in line for my TAC officer, Col. Courvoisie. When I got to his desk, he said: "Why do you want to leave this fine institution, Schreiber?"

I had rehearsed my answer: "Sir, I find military life incompatible with academic pursuits."

Before I could go on with my prepared speech, he replied: "Bullshit. It was good enough for your brother. This experience will make a man out of you. You can become a second lieutenant in this glorious United States Army!"

My mind drifted. I felt like a failure, but I also felt proud of leaving. I could turn my back on this incredible racism and not participate in it.

I repeated to Colonel Courvoisie: "I still want to resign from this institution."

He threw me the papers and shooed me out. I took my duffel bag and hopped a cab to the Fort Sumter Hotel, where I got a bottle of Scotch and drank it alone, feeling free but depressed. I'd wasted my parents' money and accomplished nothing. The next day I took a plane home to New York.

The Citadel had a room with the names inscribed of all alumni veterans killed in our wars. Of those who died in Vietnam, there was my brother's roommate, Ben Kelly.

Larry with Little Larry

Little Larry

'm not going to write about medical school, except to say that somehow I landed at State University of New York at Buffalo Medical School, where the wind came off Lake Erie at twenty below and nothing you wore helped and you could pile on jacket, sweater, gloves, and socks and still feel as if you were living in an icebox.

I remember leaving gross anatomy lab one time and walking across the frigid campus to the parking lot, a ten-minute walk. When I got to my 1961 gold Pontiac Catalina convertible, I realized I'd forgotten my keys in the lab. I had to make a quick decision: Go back across the arctic parking lot, to retrieve my keys, or lie down and freeze to death. Swear to God, it felt like a real decision! Of course, I got the damn keys.

Looking back, the numbing cold probably helped to prepare me for doctoring, which is by definition harsh. But something else transpired during medical school that would also define my life: becoming a father.

My first experience of fatherhood did not turn out well. I was a fourth-year medical student working in the Pediatric Ward at the Buffalo Children's Hospital, New York, when I first met Larry Frazier. I was 24, and 'little' Larry was 17. A hemophiliac, he was repeatedly admitted after being beaten by his father. Brown hair, blue eyes, a handsome boy but thin and pale. To me he looked like an all-American kid, a kind of Huck Finn, except this one was from the working-class steel district of Lackawanna.

Little Larry had less than 1 percent of the essential clotting factor 8 and was subjected to spontaneous bleeds into his joints and muscles. He'd wake up with a bleed without trauma—and then suffer deeper trauma when his father beat him. Then he'd bleed profusely. Even so, he had an impish grin and a joy for living. When I was assigned to his case, Carol, my first wife, was his recreation therapist. We both fell in love with this kid. We knew nothing about special-needs parenting. We thought love alone could 'fix' anyone.

When I graduated in May of 1972, Carol and I took Little Larry with us. We drove across the country in our Volkswagen van to Albuquerque, New Mexico, where I was to begin my internship at the University of New Mexico Hospital. I had picked New Mexico because it seemed like a countercultural thing to do. Hippies had been joining communes there while I was in medical school. Why not see what the state was like? Go West, Larry!

We were allowed to take Little Larry with us, because at the time, there was no foster-care supervision. Once kids were placed-in-care, as it was called, they were 'out of sight, out of mind.' So we became Little Larry's foster parents. There was no training or home study. The social worker met us at Buffalo Children's Hospital, we signed some papers, and off we went.

The three of us camped out along the way. Once, outside Little Rock, Arkansas, Little Larry woke up with a swollen elbow, a hemarthrosis. He needed an immediate infusion of Factor 8. I inserted the IV into his arm. People in the campground walked by us, curious or frightened. I had long hair and a beard; I didn't look 'like a doctor.' They must have thought we were shooting up drugs.

After two weeks, we finally reached Albuquerque. We settled into a small house in Cedar Crest, in the mountains above Albuquerque. Little Larry slept in an alcove off the living room. Carol and I thought we were 'rescuing' him.

"I miss Lackawanna," he said.

"Why?" I would ask.

"I miss my father, too."

"But he beats you."

"But he's my father."

Before long all hell exploded. After two turbulent months—coming home late, cursing, not taking showers, all sorts of conflicts—I got the phone bill: Little Larry had placed $200 worth of phone calls to New York. I was making $7,200 a year as an intern—which came out to about a dollar an hour because I worked 80 to 100 hours a week.

The breaking point was when we found his writings and sexual musings about Carol. That did it. We drove him to the airport in Albuquerque, and all three of us cried the cries of heartbreak and relief.

Postscript: Eighteen years later, Little Larry's wife called to tell us that he was dying of AIDS, which he'd contracted from all his transfusions. His wife told me that he had always talked about his time in New Mexico as "the happiest of his life." Well, his truth was different than my truth. For many years, I felt I had failed Little Larry. So perhaps the real truth shimmered somewhere in between.

New Mexico

"The Mountain will either accept you or spit you out."
Old Taos expression, quoted by everybody, accepted by few.

Doctoring for the
Indian Health Service–
Joe Shorty's Curse

After interning in Albuquerque, I began life as a rural doctor in the barren, semi-arid region just south of the city. I was 26 years old and had become enthralled and impressed by Native American culture. One particular episode involving Navajo Indians has stuck in my mind.

Navajo parents would leave their ill children at the hospital in Albuquerque for treatment and return to their reservation to take care of their other children. There was no way of contacting them, as most had no phones. Nevertheless, when we were ready to discharge a child the parents would invariably show up at the hospital exactly on the right day. It felt like magic.

Because of my interest in Native American culture, I thought it would be fun and fulfilling to work for the Indian Health Service. So I applied for a position with the service and, having been accepted, became the doctor for Isleta Pueblo.

Although assigned to the Pueblo, my responsibilities also required me to travel each Thursday to Cañoncito, a small Navajo reservation 50 miles west of Albuquerque. The Navajo there were supposedly descendants of the Cañoncito Navajo who had scouted for the U.S. Cavalry during the latter part of the 19th century. For this transgression they were scorned by the remainder of the Navajo Nation, and their portion of the reservation remained isolated from the larger reservation.

At Cañoncito I found that life was hard, at best. There was extreme poverty. Alcoholism and child neglect were rampant.

My assistant was Lucille Knudsen, a public-health nurse. She was a 55-year-old lifer from Minnesota who had started working in the Indian Health Service in 1950. She was smug, bored, and condescending, but she knew every hogan on the reservation.

On the hot Thursday afternoon in 1973 when I met Shorty, 'Nurse Ratched' asked me to go on a home visit with her. On our way out of the two-room adobe clinic, we passed through the waiting room. As usual, it was full of kids with green mucus dripping from their noses or pus oozing from their ears because of ruptured eardrums caused by untreated infections. On the wall, someone had put up a large poster of the Point Reyes Beach in Northern California. It showed turquoise water, blue sky, and golden sand. The mothers of the children sat staring at the poster as we left, just as they had been doing all day.

Going east on dirt roads, we dodged potholes that could swallow our government-issued 1965 Chevy station wagon. After passing an assortment of hogans and trailers, we arrived at the Yazzie hogan. Mrs. Yazzie invited me in, careful not to be rude by making eye contact. Her hogan was one room, with a woodburning stove. Her husband, Frank, was lying on a bed against the curved wall, having just had a grand mal seizure.

Mrs. Yazzie and I, eyes downcast, said nothing, but we understood each other. Frank had stopped drinking 48 hours earlier, whereupon the gods played their usual cruel trick reserved for alcoholics. When heavy drinkers try to stop drinking, instead of immediately feeling better they suffer withdrawal seizures and hallucinations, delirium tremens (DTs).

As I was examining Mr. Yazzie, it started to hail. In New Mexico, a hailstorm can really get your attention, especially when it involves (as it often does) hailstones the size of golf balls. While I attended to her husband, Mrs. Yazzie quietly took out her broom and calmly swept the hailstones out their doorless home. The ferocity of the hailstorm startled us all, including Maria, the community health representative and translator who had arrived shortly before the storm.

Translations have always frustrated me. I would ask a question like, "Does it hurt after a fatty meal?" whereupon Maria and the patient would confer for two minutes. About half the time, both of them would look down, not answering the question. Then I would ask, trying to appear patient and laid back, "Well, Maria, does it hurt after he eats?" Maria would say something to the patient briefly in Diné Bizaad (Navajo language), and the patient would finally say, "No." Translations left me in the dark, and I'd always wonder if the patient was actually answering my question or whether the two of them were saying, "Can you believe this? He's a doctor and he gets paid for this!"

Additionally, I found out later from Maria that as Mrs. Yazzie was sweeping the hailstones out of her hogan, she told Maria that Joe Shorty had called down the hailstorm. Exactly who Joe Shorty was I never discovered, but he had a reputation for being a miserable human being, an alcoholic child molester. Yet the Cañoncito Navajo also believed that he possessed special powers. In short, he was a sort of shadowy, shamanic character I would never meet. Mrs. Yazzie was convinced that Joe Shorty, though dead, had called down the storm in revenge for some past offense. "This hailstorm is part of Joe Shorty's curse," she told Maria.

Through Maria, I told Mrs. Yazzie not to worry, that I would take care of her family despite Joe Shorty's 'magic.' Having reassured her, my next concern was to get Mr. Yazzie to the Albuquerque Indian Hospital.

At that time, there was only one phone on the reservation and it was an eight-person party line. Mrs. Yazzie didn't have a phone, or running water for that matter.

Since the Cañoncito clinic phone was one of the eight lines, I decided to drive back there in order to call the hospital and make sure there was a bed for Mr. Yazzie. Thirty minutes later, driving the old station wagon, which didn't have an air conditioner, inhaling dust with every breath, I made it back to the clinic. I walked past the still-waiting mothers and children, peeked at the Point Reyes picture, and picked up the phone to call the hospital.

A panicked voice broke into the party line, "A tornado has destroyed Mrs. Yazzie's hogan and has lifted the roof off Daniel Morningstar's trailer!"

I thought about Daniel on my drive back to the disaster. A friendly but paranoid schizophrenic, Daniel never took his meds. Once a month, Lucille gave him a Prolixin Decanoate shot, a long-acting antipsychotic juice. I wondered what Morningstar imagined had happened to him. Did he believe in Joe Shorty's curse? What did he think, being isolated and schizophrenic, when his roof was blown off by a huge wind? I only know that Daniel was not seen or heard from for six weeks. When he eventually showed up for his next Prolixin shot, he was calmer and less psychotic than ever.

Back to that Thursday. I drove back to the disaster. In the rubble, I found Mrs. Yazzie's granddaughter, hand outstretched, cold and motionless. This little one still had her flattened occiput from the cradleboard. The dead child's mother was lying near, vomiting and weeping and complaining of numbness of her legs. I did what I could with what I had: inserted IVs in Mrs. Yazzie's daughter and three other injured people. Mrs. Yazzie's daughter had just lost her child and was in danger of dying herself. Her left upper quadrant was rigid, her spleen most likely ruptured, blood filling her abdominal cavity. I started a second IV in her other arm to keep her blood pressure stable and poured in the saline.

The ever-dependable Lucille drove the station wagon back to the clinic and called an Albuquerque ambulance. They got lost. The Laguna and Acoma EMTs did not respond. So one hour later, I loaded four bleeding people and one dead child into the back of my station wagon and drove to Albuquerque with the IV bottles hanging outside the window, the bottles held high by Lucille who used gravity's help to increase the IV flow rate. Nobody spoke or prayed (at least not out loud). No one moaned. There was only me calling periodically for Lucille to give me vital signs. I drove straight to the ER at the trauma center at the university hospital and unloaded my patients.

That night, I turned on the news and learned that tornados hardly ever struck west of the Rio Grande and that 46 people had been injured. I went from exhausted to exhilarated to totally insecure. 46? I'd dropped off only four injured and one dead. I imagined 42 people buried under the rubble, shouting, "Stupid white man." Was this Joe Shorty's curse? Did he, as Mrs. Yazzie had hinted, cause the tornado? There were so many things I didn't know or believe. However, when I called the ER, I learned that no one else had been hurt: The newsman had meant to say four to six injured.

I went to bed cursing Joe Shorty.

Psych Ward

The phone rang at 3 a.m. in the sterile government house, where I was deep in an exhausted sleep. At the time, working without rest was a testing ground for doctors—a medical macho attitude passed on from generation to generation of doctors in training. But it led to poor patient care. I got out of bed and stumbled to the phone.

"Yes?"

A nurse responded, "Doctor, we need you to pronounce a patient."

Throwing on scrubs, I zigzagged across the street to the New Mexico State Hospital in Las Vegas, where I served as the sole doctor for 500 psychotic patients. The year was 1973, and I still lived outside Albuquerque and worked at the Isleta Pueblo for the Indian Health Services. And I continued to visit Cañoncito every Thursday. But with two children and a third on the way, it didn't quite pay the bills. So one weekend a month, I left my family and traveled 120 miles northeast to the only state psychiatric hospital in 120,000 square miles. In those days, they kept the state hospitals far away from the population centers, like prisons. Out of sight, out of mind.

The drive to Las Vegas, New Mexico, was gorgeous. I'd ride my Honda CB350 motorcycle through the picturesque villages of Golden and Madrid, the pink evening light mesmerizing. The sun would set as I crossed the railroad tracks in Galisteo, where the landscape was dotted with old adobe homes, horses, and cows—all of which stood against a background of golden brush.

The charge nurse pointed me to the room. An old woman lay there, mouth open, looking like she died twenty years ago. I leaned over her bed, placed my stethoscope on her chest, and listened for an audible heartbeat. I was so tired I couldn't tell if *I* was alive, much less a 90-year-old long-term resident. After listening for what seemed like an hour, the same nurse leaned in the room and gasped.

"Not that one, Doctor!" she said. "The patient in the next bed!"

After pronouncing the dead one officially dead, my diagnosis right on the money this time, I asked if I could call the deceased's family. The nurse didn't feel this was a required part of our job but threw me a chart anyway. I studied it for ten minutes and learned that the patient had been committed for promiscuity by her rancher parents in 1932. From what I could tell, she wasn't crazy when she was admitted. But after 40 years of institutionalization, she certainly became so.

As I dialed the number, the nurse casually said, "That's the wrong chart, Doctor." I hung up as the next of kin for the wrong patient answered the phone.

Mistaken charts. Forgotten people. At 26, I was full of good intentions but had virtually no psychiatric experience except for a month rotation in medical school and one month in my internship. I worked Friday nights to Sunday nights, running on roughly four hours of sleep. I sutured the fingers of patients that had been bitten off by other, even crazier, patients. When I walked down the sterile hallways with the all-important keys, hordes of them followed me, and I'd lead them from one locked ward into the next locked ward, misplacing them for others to find. All for $300 a weekend—and I thought I was extorting the state, for that was more money than I made per week in my regular job at the Indian Health Service.

But sometimes I left to go to the movies. There were no beepers or cell phones in those days. The nurse told me, "Don't worry, we'll contact you." How? I wondered.

One night in downtown Las Vegas, watching a Charles Bronson flick, suddenly, on the screen, a handwritten note appeared: "Dr. Schreiber, a phone call." Another evening, I was at the drive-in when through the speaker by the car window (and everyone else's) came a voice: "Dr. Schreiber, phone call."

————————

I worked at the Psych Ward—yes—for the money, as well as for the experience. Yet, I was totally responsible for the care of so many people! I'd write orders admitting patients on Thorazine, choose an arbitrary dose, and hope the psychiatrist (there was only one) would modify it in a few days. A month later, not only were the patients on the same dose, but they hadn't been seen by the shrink at all. These patients were all indigent people, and the state contributed only limited funds and limited care to take care of people with unlimited needs.

One morning, I was called to see Mr. Pacheco, a mentally challenged young man with lymph-node enlargement and an enlarged spleen. I knew from examining him and from simple lab work that he had a lymphoma of some sort. I called the administrator, who lived in town, and asked if this patient could be transferred to the University of New Mexico Hospital in Albuquerque. It was Sunday, and the administrator pacified me by telling me they would send him to the university on Monday, when they were fully staffed. Weeks later, I came back and Mr. Pacheco was still languishing in the same ward.

On a typical weekend, I'd admit ten new schizophrenics from all over the state. I was also responsible for the twenty-bed medical ward of mentally ill patients who were ill enough physically to be sent to that ward. Some of the patients were incapable of giving me a history. I was also the doctor for the Meadows Nursing Home Facility down the road. To add to the frenzy, I was medically responsible for the criminally insane in the forensic unit.

As you can imagine, or perhaps you can't, the work petrified me. A Mr. Gonzales had been committed in the 1920s, when there were no psychiatrists in any rural areas and probably very few even in Albuquerque, New Mexico's largest city. His chart included the official papers committing him to the state hospital. Among these papers was the decree by a judge in accordance with the recommendations of a general practitioner: "We find Mr. Gonzales insane, secondary to excessive masturbation."

It seemed to me then, and I still believe now, that this hospital was a place where people were committed because they didn't fit in. Or because they were troubled and became psychotic. Or where psychotic people become more psychotic.

The deinstitutionalization of mental health in the late '60s and '70s seemed a noble gesture. Its goal was to reintegrate psychiatric patients into their communities. The hope was that with the new medications and community health centers, the thousands of patients who had languished in state hospitals would be free to reenter society.

However, many of those released were without family, without community support, without resources. Those without support simply drifted into the swelling population of the homeless. We still face this situation today, 40 years later. We decreed that all psychiatric patients needed to be treated at home. Whose home? Which patients?

Larry, early 70's, west of Albuquerque

Cords of Wood

After my two-year stint at the Indian Health Service, I needed a job. And I wanted to stay in New Mexico. So I called Mike Kaufman, my chief resident in internal medicine in 1972. He had opened a practice in Taos. He was running a grant for the Questa Health Center, a federally designated shortage area. That meant they needed more physicians.

The clinic in Questa was situated between mountains—flaming red mountains at sunset on the east, and the vast high desert on the west. Our small staff often went to the Rio Grande Gorge for lunch at La Junta, the junction where the Red River joins the Rio Grande. You'd look down 800 feet to the river-valley floor, and you'd actually see a line where the Red River, clear green, merged with the muddy brown Rio Grande.

Other times, we'd eat at Louie's, a greasy spoon with four tables covered with plastic tablecloths, white with faded flowers. Five of us would come in, and Louie, in the kitchen, would never come out. We ordered French fries, burritos, and sopaipillas fried in grease. Not exactly the low-fat food that we doctors now recommend to our patients. Louie died of heart disease. Our only other choice was the El Seville, another greasy spoon, the only difference being that it was larger.

The Questa clinic was a prefab modular building with four exam rooms, an emergency room, a waiting room; and I had an office with the view of the mountains. I loved it, loved the whole lifestyle. I knew every-body, and at home I had chickens and my kids (by this time I had three) ran around naked.

Our log cabin was in San Cristobal, about eight miles south of Questa. It was one room, divided by sheet rock into two. Later, we added a bedroom above the main room. The log cabin had only a woodburn-ing stove, which we both cooked on and used for heat. Our house had no insulation. We were also on an eight-person party line. Sometimes when I needed to call the hospital, Simon Gonzales would be on the phone talk-ing to his girlfriend. We'd argue.

"Simon, I need to call the hospital."

"I'm talkin' to my girlfriend, call later."

Eventually, and only when he wanted to, he'd hang up.

During the next 15 years, my household would mushroom from three to 13 children. We outgrew the log cabin and built a large home on the creek, with two ponds and mighty cottonwood trees all around. We still used woodburning stoves for heat. One wood stove in the playroom heated all the bedrooms; the other heated the living room, dining room, and kitchen. During the winter, I would get up at four a.m. to add wood to the smoldering embers. When my older children went to college, and stayed at friends' homes with thermostats, they said they were amazed that the heat could be turned on with a flick of the dial! They thought 'normal' was eating breakfast standing up in front of the stove, shaking and dressed in their winter jackets. It seemed so much colder in those days.

Taos is one of the poorest counties in New Mexico, and New Mexico is one of the poorest states in the country. So there I was running the clinic in Questa. I was doing a lot of obstetric work, and the women who had partners could not afford health insurance or qualify for Medicaid. But I never had to buy a cord of wood. Men would drop off cords of wood in payment for a birth, or extended hospitalization, or for a gall bladder, hernia, or appendectomy. I would assist the surgeon and the next week find a cord of wood left stacked at my house.

Wood wasn't all I traded for. Without trading I wouldn't have a barn (OB and tubal ligation), a chicken coop and goat pen (delivery of a baby), or fencing throughout my fields (pneumonia and gall bladder attack). I even traded medical care for house cleaning. How else do you keep a house clean with 13 children? Trading felt good. It worked.

Mr. Jablonski

I t was my fault. It began, appropriately enough, with pity. Pity for Police Chief William Taggart. Chief Taggart had that Don Knotts quality about him—all five feet six inches and 115 pounds of him—with one of the worst essential tremors I had ever seen. Not too appealing for the sole law-enforcement officer in the small town of Questa, elevation 7,500 feet, population 1,000, in the heart of the Sangre de Cristo Mountains of Northern New Mexico. Doing his annual physical for the police academy, I was to make sure he qualified physically and endurance-wise. But the chief whined that his back was out and he could not do the required number of push-ups and sit-ups. "But gee doc, I need the job."

Young and wanting to please, I took the low road and passed him on his physical. After all, who needed a macho cop in this idyllic place? Only a few hippies got beat up occasionally at the Kiowa Lounge in Questa. In other parts of Taos County, things got more heated.

A few days later, the EMTs brought a Mr. Jablonski into the Questa Health Center, where I was now the chief doctor. Just the week before, I'd lectured the medics on "Handling the Combative Patient." Oh, how I loved to teach and be center stage in those days. So when the medics brought in Mr. Jablonski—with an accompanying report describing a potentially dangerous and psychotic patient—I took it as an opportunity to teach and shine. Astutely, I sized him up, realizing something was not quite right; this wild-haired Eastern European was hallucinating. I looked at his eyes and noticed his glasses lacked one important component: lenses. Obviously paranoid schizophrenic, he was rambling in English and Polish, obsessing about his hemorrhoids, but wouldn't allow me within three feet of his anal varicosities.

Remembering a prior patient, my trusted LPN, Eloisa Cisneros, asked if she should summon 'the Polish translator.' Knowing Mrs. Shukavitz lived 20 miles north in Costilla on the Colorado line, and as a full-time maid, I doubted she had expertise with psychotic, eyeglass-lenseless men with bleeding hemorrhoids. I shook my head.

Jablonski became more restless. I couldn't help noticing the EMTs over my shoulder. I enjoyed the attention and looked forward to a satisfactory resolution. Jablonski kept on about his hemorrhoids and his need for psychic healing—not to include a proctoscopic examination.

Then I summed it up. "Well, Mr. Jablonski, I think you need a hospital."

"Yes," Jablonski enthusiastically concurred.

"And a hospital that can treat your hemorrhoids and your justifiable emotional needs," I added.

Jablonski nodded, agreeing with every word.

"Therefore, the best hospital is the New Mexico State Psychiatric Hospital just over the pass in Las Vegas." Again, Jablonski nodded at my suggestion as if they were written on slate.

"And finally, since you have no car, our gentle Police Chief William Taggart will gladly transport you."

A final nod and a smile from my patient and admiring glances from the audience of two EMTs.

Chief Taggart was summoned. Minutes later, he nervously pulled into the parking lot of the Questa Health Center. Just then Jablonski started to unravel, waving his arms and shaking his head back and forth.

Just a little bump in the road, I thought. Cocky and self-assured, I tried to calm down the actively hallucinating visiting Pole, who seemed poised to charge our hyperthyroid chief of police.

"Now Mr. Jablonski, don't get upset, no one will hurt you," I assured him.

Jablonski's eyes bulged out. Then almost too calmly he pronounced, "The only one that will get hurt is you, doctor."

With that statement he grabbed Taggart's billy club and went after me. I took off across the parking lot, running as fast as my transported New York legs would carry me. It was my first wind sprint since running track in the ninth grade. Jablonski threw the lead-lined club and caught me square in my right gluteus maximus; luckily, this was the only place on my body that would not break. I continued to run. Don't worry, I thought, the police are here! Then Chief Taggart took out his revolver and aimed. I turned and watched with horror: This under-qualified testosterone-deficient cop, who only passed his physical by my dishonesty, was aiming a gun, his arm shaking.

I yelled, "Don't shoot, Chief!" sure that he would miss the psychotic Pole and kill the neurotic Jew instead. Taggart lowered his gun and, realizing his own capabilities, did what he did best—nothing.

Hands shaking, I opened the door to my truck, climbed in, and attempted to start the engine. As I did so, Jablonski, having reclaimed the club, jumped on the hood and was about to smash in the windshield. Then, just as abruptly as he'd gone berserk, as if hearing one of my ancestors creeping into his hallucinations pleading for mercy, Jablonski dropped the club and departed gingerly, almost daintily, from the hood of my truck. Taggart, ever the opportunist, sprang back into action and handcuffed the now passive suspect and saved the day.

I limped back to the clinic. The EMTs patted my back. Ms. Cisneros smiled. I smiled back, wondering what I would say in my next lecture on handling the combative patient.

It Takes All Types

On most days, my patients were Northern New Mexico Hispanics. Their families had lived in the area for 400 years. The elderly spoke solely Spanish; the younger Hispanics were bilingual.

I worked all day at the clinic and sometimes all night at the Holy Cross Hospital in Taos. One evening, while making rounds at the hospital, I visited a *viejita*, an elderly woman, who had pneumonia. I was talking nonstop, telling her about her condition, thinking she understood; it was her alert face, bright eyes, small smile. But to make sure, I asked her family members there if they thought she knew who I was.

"She's not understanding what's going on, Dr. Schreiber."

"Does she know who I am?"

They asked in Spanish, "Who is the man speaking to you?"

The *viejita* replied in what I assumed was a competent way, because she looked so attentive. But the family laughed.

"What is so funny?" I asked.

"She said, *'La esposa del líder de la banda.'* You are the band leader's wife."

I cracked up. I was hardly the perfect image of a doctor. I had grown a huge mustache and let my hair frizz into a bulky 'fro that doubled the size of my head. I wore baggy Levis and a cowboy shirt with pearl buttons. I had on a pair of broken-down cowboy boots. So I guess you could say I was responsible for the *viejita's* confusion.

Back in the clinic the next day, my next patient was a middle-aged Hispanic miner. Luckily he spoke very good English. I introduced myself and asked, "How can I help?"

"Just give me a shot of penicillin, doc, and I will be on my way."

"What makes you think you need a shot of penicillin?"

"Because that is what old Dr. Thomas does in La Jara whenever I have a sore throat." La Jara was 40 miles to the northwest.

"Well, let's take a look," I said.

I examined the man carefully, checking for fever and looking for pus on the tonsils, hemorrhagic spots indicative of strep, a swollen uvula (the bell that hangs down from your palate), or swollen lymph nodes. He had none of the signs that would have suggested strep or justified penicillin. His throat was pink. I spent the next five minutes explaining the difference between viruses and bacteria. I told him he had a virus and that a virus doesn't need penicillin. In fact if we do give a patient penicillin haphazardly, we not only don't help the patient, we create resistant bacteria.

He was not impressed. I told him I would do a throat culture and if it turned out positive for the strep bacteria, I would gladly give him his penicillin. He looked at me with disdain, turned around and left. I suspect that he probably drove up to La Jara and got his shot.

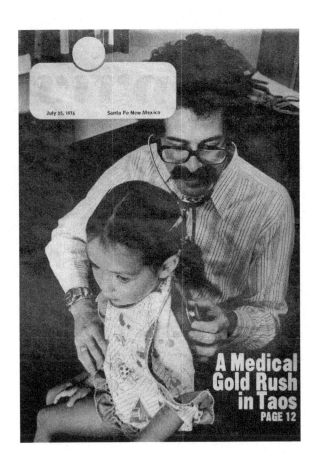

July 25, 1976   Santa Fe New Mexico

A Medical
Gold Rush
in Taos
PAGE 12

That same hot day in July of 1976, waiting patiently in an examining room at the clinic was a bone-thin young man with long scraggly hair that hadn't been washed in weeks. "How can I help you?" He couldn't speak; he was drooling. He had trismus, the inability to open his mouth. Most of the time it was caused when a person's tonsils were enlarged and inflamed. The boy took out his pen and wrote on a crumpled piece of paper, "I have a sore throat."

I took his temperature; it was 104. His lymph nodes were swollen. And when I forced his mouth open, he had what we call 'kissing tonsils'—so swollen they touched. His were full of pus and he was in danger of a peritonsillar abscess.

When I informed him that he needed a shot of procaine penicillin to prevent hospitalization, he responded by writing: "Isn't that a bit drastic for my immune system? Can't we do a throat culture and treat it with 'natural' herbs and the like?" After I bluntly explained to him that his natural remedy was likely to result in his natural death, he reluctantly agreed to the penicillin. I realized that I was in a unique, sometimes crazy, but always interesting community.

One of the nicest features of our 'interesting' community involved a custom followed by Hispanic women. When they came to the clinic, they often would bring a tin of biscochitos for 'Doctor Larry.'

The generosity of the women was matched by the courage of their husbands. When I would tell one of them that they had a terminal illness, he would usually respond: "Well, Doc, everybody has to die." Perhaps it was their deep Catholic faith, their belief on an afterlife, or perhaps it was a matter of honor, a determination to show no weakness or fear. I felt I had something to learn from them. Did they understand something about the cycle of life that I had yet to learn?

Many of the men worked at the molybdenum mine in Questa. The mine brought financial security, even though it denuded the mountains and polluted the Red River. Much of the community lived in their self-built adobe homes with wood heat, down dirt roads inaccessible from snowpack in winter and often inaccessible from mud in the spring.

One time, my well-trusted paramedic, Lawrence Cisneros, and I were driving the ambulance down such a road to pick up a very ill Geneva Montoya, a 90-year-old woman living in Cerro. We got to the end of the only road in Cerro, went inside the house, and attempted to resuscitate this frail, osteoporotic woman. We placed her on a stretcher, lifted her into the ambulance, and continued our attempts to revive her. We were not successful; she died in the ambulance, in front of the house she was born in.

Since we already had her body, we thought we'd help the family by transporting her directly to the funeral home. As we tried to drive out, we found we were stuck in foot-deep, typical New Mexico spring mud. Almost casually, and not intentionally, I mentioned to Lawrence that we needed more 'dead weight.' We looked at each other and shared that common bond that crosses cultures: laughter—in the face of this regrettable death of a family matriarch.

During my early years in Taos, there were two traffic lights: one at the Plaza and another one, the blinking light at the intersection of Highway 522 and Ski Valley Road. We had a food co-op in Taos, and Rael's 'supermarket' in Questa carried canned goods, rice, and beans. There was also the Safeway in Taos. We went shopping for bulk foods in Santa Fe and clothes in Albuquerque.

San Cristobal was a farming community that seemed, for most of the time, harmonious and peaceful—mostly because of one woman, Jenny Vincent. She'd moved to San Cristobal to study with Frieda Lawrence, the wife of English novelist D.H. Lawrence. Jenny and her husband, Craig, started a ranch, San Cristobal Valley Ranch.

Both Jenny and Craig were activists. Jenny was a well-known folksinger, who had sung with Pete Seeger and accompanied Paul Robeson on the piano. In 1947, teaching Spanish in the local schools was prohibited. In response to this prohibition, Jenny and Mrs. Baca, a local school teacher, visited classrooms and sang songs in Spanish, even though it was against the law.

Jenny had been my next-door neighbor for 39 years when she recently moved into the Taos Retirement Village. At 102, she is still as alert as when I first met her almost 40 years ago and delights in playing the piano for residents of the center. Unfortunately, there were other Anglos who were far less simpatico than Jenny. There was Mrs. Golden, who ran the General Store (yes, it was called General Store). She took advantage of the situation that developed when so many men in our community were off fighting in World War II. Because of the absence of fathers, husbands, sons, and brothers, local women became so strapped for money that they were forced to trade their lands for food. Mrs. Golden, and a few other opportunist types, thus gained acres of land, and lots of mistrust. Soon thereafter, the expression *'no vender la tierra'* (do not sell the land) was painted on boulders throughout the canyon. What happened in San Cristobal and Questa happened throughout Taos County. And the local cultures are still fuming about it to this day.

In the '60s, Taos became a favored destination for hippies. Ranging from New York 'trustafarians' to California surfers, they had come to New Mexico in search of a different lifestyle. Most of them were drawn to the few communes that existed around Taos, including New Buffalo, in Arroyo Hondo; the commune at Lorien, north of Questa; and the Hog Farm, near Peñasco, located on the southern end of Taos County.

A popular retreat was the Lama Foundation, located at the foot of Flag Mountain, just above the town of La Lama, an old Hispanic village five miles north of my home in San Cristobal. Until 1964, the highway ended at San Cristobal. Greyhound buses drove along the dirt roads in my village and came out—if they made it—on the highway at La Lama, a few miles south of Questa.

By the time I ran the Questa Clinic, the Lama Foundation was going full blast, offering a spiritual path for anyone who sought it. Young people came there seeking enlightenment—if only for a short time.

———

At night, I worked at Holy Cross Hospital in Taos, where I took care of people too sick to be treated as outpatients. One of my responsibilities was to back up the midwives if their out-of-hospital-births ran into complications. The midwives were dedicated and much nicer than us (the doctors). The two main midwives were Elizabeth Gilmore and Tish Denim. Both women are gone now, but they served the community for decades. Elizabeth was so sweet I couldn't get irritated at her even though she usually called me at 4 a.m. Her diagnoses were usually right on, and she was not afraid to seek traditional allopathic medical help for her patients.

One evening in the ER, she brought in a patient who had a retained placenta and was bleeding profusely. I poured the IV fluids into her and manually removed most of the placenta using a curette to get out what was left. Elizabeth held the healthy newborn boy, and then gasped as the baby turned white and the blanket was suddenly saturated with blood. The midwives didn't use a plastic clamp on the umbilical cord but instead usually tied the cord with a sterile string. The string had unraveled. I grabbed a large metal clamp and shut off the blood flow from the umbilical cord. I was pretty proud of myself. I thought I saved two people that night. Yet I guess I was a reminder to the new mother of her failure to give birth 'naturally' at home. When I discharged her from the hospital, she wouldn't look me in the eye. That newborn is now married to a nurse.

One morning in Questa, Esther, a young woman from the Lama Foundation came in with her colicky baby. "Is this because I've done something wrong?" she asked me.

"Colic is tough for any mother to deal with. It's not a maternal shortcoming. In no way is it your fault," I answered in my best doctor voice.

She decided the only thing that would quiet her two-month-old was a teaspoon of honey. Since the Questa Honey Farm was next door, she left the clinic and went there for the cure. There was one huge problem with this. Just the previous year, a report out of California stated that some infants who were fed honey could not detoxify the spores that produced botulism toxin. Adults had no problem. But for infants it could cause sudden death.

At the time, many infant deaths attributed to SIDS were actually resulting from a paralysis caused by botulism toxin. Once children reach the age of six to twelve months, they can detoxify the botulism.

Patiently (I thought), I explained this to her. But she argued that honey was natural and good. I argued, "You wouldn't give your child Diet Coke would you?"

"Of course not," she replied.

"I wouldn't either. Giving your child Diet Coke might kill him in twenty years, while this honey might kill him tonight!"

On another occasion, an elderly woman with crippling rheumatoid arthritis asked me to use a bee to sting her inflamed joint, a folk remedy that was presumed to lessen the pain and inflammation. What is a good doctor to do?

Each week, I went next door to the honey farm. Here, I picked up a bee with a surgical pickup (in your heart, you know I'm talking 'bout tweezers). Upon returning to the clinic, I would plant it on her proximal phalangeal joint. The bee would sting her and she did feel better—probably from all the cortisol and epinephrine her adrenals produced in reaction to the sting. However, after a while she came back in with cellulitis (a soft-tissue skin infection) due to her reaction to the stings—so I stopped doing that procedure.

Another time, I was asked to do a ritual circumcision at the Lama Foundation, which was loaded with Sufi followers, Hindus, Jewish kids, and others—all whom were seeking a spiritual path. In a small, unlit hut, I performed the circumcision with a flashlight as the sunlight slowly faded.

While I was trying to use the last rays of the sun coming in through the only window, a friend of the parents was praying, OM OM OM, and was so moved that he rocked back and forth, intermittently blocking the light from the window, which played havoc with the lighting in the "surgical field." I was sure that in this semidarkness I would amputate the tip of this poor little infant's penis. Luckily, he lived to pee and have erections. I never did a circumcision there again.

Time for a Change

Why is it that I remember so well the early days of practicing medicine? It's not because I am demented; at least I don't think that's the reason. It is because the earliest days were so exciting. Everything was new and I had so much responsibility and everything was fresh and stimulating. I remember like it was last week my time in the Questa Clinic from 1976 to 1980. I loved teaching then and almost always had a medical student to bring along. Sometimes they got in the way and were irritating, but I formed life-long friendships with a few of them—like Bill Garlick, a super-bright med student who was forever asking stimulating questions. We shared an experience that fortunately turned out OK.

One day, the clinic got a call from a patient's mother. Her daughter, Veronica Montoya, was gurgling and her lungs were filling up with fluids. "She can't breathe. Help us!"

Veronica had lupus, along with kidney and lung disease, and could scarcely care for herself; so I knew this was an emergency situation. Since Lawrence Cisneros, our EMT and ambulance driver, was sick, I grabbed Bill and we jumped into the ambulance. I drove, my adrenalin pumping. As we rocked and rolled along, I shouted my questions to Bill on the main treatments for pulmonary edema.

It was 20 miles from Questa to Costilla, where we turned off on the dirt road to Amalia, where Veronica lived.

Medical students like mnemonics. For pulmonary edema in 1976, you spelled out MOST DAMP. M stood for *morphine;* O for *oxygen;* S for *sit up;* T for *tourniquets,* to cut off the blood supply to the heart and the lungs; D for *digitalis;* A for *aminophylline;* M for *mercuhydrin,* an old diuretic no longer used; P for *IPPB,* a breathing treatment. Whew! Looking back at this mnemonic, it's as if we were in the dark ages, with leeches and phlebotomies (the letting of blood).

In front of us was a typical New Mexico pickup going 35 miles an hour, even though the speed limit was 55. I put on the siren and sped past him. My pulse shot up. I started to sweat. "Slow down!" I told myself. When we finally got to our patient, she was in respiratory distress with rales all over her lungs, indicating the presence of fluid. She had pulmonary edema. Bill placed an oxygen mask over her mouth and nose; I started an IV and injected morphine and furosemide, a diuretic.

We lifted her into the ambulance. I let Bill drive so I could be in the back with my patient. On the hill in Arroyo Hondo, her stretcher began zigzagging across the ambulance. I had to grab it like a cowboy grabs a steer. I had forgotten to lock it in. By the time we arrived in Taos, Veronica was blue-cyanotic; the oxygen tank empty. We raced to Holy Cross Hospital, where she was put in what we then called the monitor bed (we had no ICU). A nurse would be with her at all times. She survived. Bill and I still talk about that day when we madly drove the ambulance and, happily, didn't kill anyone on the road. And we helped a patient.

By December of 1979, though, I was fed up with the bureaucracy that went along with running a federally funded clinic. For example, I had requested another doctor, even part time. I was working 12 hours a day and on call every night. I drove to the Denver Federal Office, where I pleaded my case to a 'suit.' The suit told me: "You don't have enough 'encounters.'"

Encounters were visits with patients. It turned out that all 50 clinics throughout the Rocky Mountains were only outpatient care. Only at Questa did we hospitalize and treat heart attacks, congestive heart failure, and birth babies. When I stayed up all night with Jose Martinez, who suffered with an unstable heart attack, that counted as one 'encounter.' When I treated a sore throat for five minutes, that also was one encounter. I explained to the suit the difference between the two and, finally, got a part-time doctor.

But it wasn't nearly enough. The paper counting and reporting got to me. I decided to go on my own and open a practice in Taos.

My first office was on the main drag in town, in an old adobe with a fireplace in the waiting room/living room/consulting room. Two bedrooms served as examining rooms, and the microscope sat in the closet. It was slow at first, and I continued to feel itchy. I felt that I needed to do something different, something totally new—even adventurous. When I was ready to leave the Questa Clinic, I had sent an application to the International Committee of the Red Cross, volunteering to go to Cambodia.

You have to know this. In 1975, the Vietnam War, which had lasted for ten years, had finally come to an end, and thousands of U.S. soldiers were coming home. The news was full of the takeover of the American Embassy, the sight of helicopters leaving Saigon, packed with Americans and their South Vietnamese collaborators and families. As this was happening, the Khmer Rouge, who had taken power in Cambodia, emptied that country's capital, Phnom Penh, of its inhabitants. In the States, we were saturated and overloaded with Vietnam—at least I was. I remember staring at a *Time Magazine* photo of Rosalynn Carter holding a frail Cambodian child. Something about the frail child in the photo seemed to be pulling me. *Here was something I could do. I could make a difference.*

I also felt guilty for what had happened in Vietnam and Cambodia. As an American, I felt ashamed. As a doctor, I felt I could make some amends, however small my efforts may seem. However late it may have been. The Khmer Rouge, it was said, were overreacting to the bombing and invasion policies of Nixon and Kissinger, who had carpet-bombed the northern portion of Cambodia during the Vietnam War. I soon learned of their 'overreaction' through the mass killings, jailing, and executions that were destroying Cambodian culture. When the Khmer Rouge gained power, there were 50,000 Buddhist monks; by 1979 there were 500. An estimated 1.7 million Cambodians had perished.

I thought the Red Cross would respond immediately. When I didn't hear from them, I contacted church-run aid groups. One phoned me. "Would you preach in the name of Jesus?" I wasn't that crazy about my own religion—I certainly wasn't going to proselytize for theirs. So I opened my office thinking the Red Cross would never call me. After being in private practice for three months, I received a telegram. "Dr. Schreiber, would you lead a medical team on the Thai-Cambodian border for the International Committee of the Red Cross? If so, you must be in Washington in three days."

Three days later, I left my practice and headed for Southeast Asia.

Nong Chan Camp, 1980
(Rice In Her Mouth)

"Please say each skull has a voice and an appetite."
—Catherine Strisik, *Thousand-Cricket Song*

Seven in the morning—brown water buffaloes wallow in emerald-green, snake-infested rice paddies set below even greener rolling hills. The leaves on the sugar palm trees flanking our route are covered in dust caused by the constant passage of military vehicles and civilian motorcycles weighed down with whole families. Malnourished dogs bark at us.

I drive along the potholed dusty road, stopping at various Thai military checkpoints. We've been in the Red Cross Toyota pickup for about an hour, having left Aranyaprathet in Thailand, where we loaded up with the daily supply of IV fluids, antibiotics, and antimalarials. We're headed for the Nong Chan Refugee Camp, located on the Thailand-Cambodia border, a major feeding station for the 60,000 Cambodians displaced from their homeland by the Khmer Rouge. I am in the midst of the most intense three months of my life.

With me in this Red Cross pickup, with its broken air conditioner in these sweltering conditions, are five nurses. I am one of only two American doctors allowed into the border camps. All of us, even so early in the day, are soaked in sweat. The sun is blistering in this pre-monsoon season.

Larry with Ouk Damry, 1980

Just short of the camp entrance we are waved to a stop. This checkpoint is manned by six teenage soldiers of Task Force 80, a right-wing Thai military group whose function is to prevent Cambodian refugees from escaping into Thailand. They are also there to keep 'excess' aid from reaching the camp and to make the border 'unattractive' to the starving refugees. According to official reports, the Khmer Rouge killed millions of their own people—Cambodians. I would later adopt a boy from the camp—an orphan who had witnessed the death of his mother, father, and five brothers and sisters. As poet U Sam Oeur called it, "death by starvation, death by disease, and death by execution."

A skinny Thai soldier carrying a U.S.-made M16 rifle, inspects our papers. I punch on my walkie-talkie to connect with the United Nations advance person—he is the one who checks out the camp for us, radioing us information about the situation in the area. "The border is quiet, the enemy is not active today, go on in." Or, "It's too bloody dangerous right now—do not proceed."

Just as I'm about to turn on the engine, my attention is diverted. At first I don't understand. The scene makes no sense. It is surreal. A Thai soldier is aiming his rifle at a Khmer family of three: a father, mother, and child. The soldier is yelling and shooting! Can this be possible? Of course it's possible. What should I do? Get out of the car? Wave my hands? What? I do what I know best when frustrated in an automobile. I honk my horn over and over and over. I'm really leaning on it. I bang on it as hard as I can. I'm hoping it will distract the soldier. I can't speak. I keep honking.

Startled, another Thai teenage soldier swings his weapon around, jamming the M16 right into my face. I quit banging on the horn and reflexively lift my hand to push the barrel away. Cora, one of the nurses, shrieks, and Sister Marie shouts, "No!"

The soldier is apoplectic, jabbing at me, screaming epithets. I flinch, twitching. Oh god he might pull the trigger! Just then, a Thai superior officer hustles over to us, barking orders in Thai and English: "Move now—leave, Red Cross people." He grabs my assailant's shoulder, yanking him away. Breathless, ears ringing, hands shaking, I fumble to start the pickup. I hope our presence will prevent bloodshed, but we still hear shots being fired. I stall twice, then drive forward into the refugee camp.

When we enter the camp, the banner over the entrance pisses me off more than usual: Welcome Thai Khmer Friendship Nong Chan Camp. The nurses and I stumble out of the truck. Damry hurries over, clearly agitated. Damry, a 'barefoot doctor,' speaks a moderate amount of French and English. I trained him, and we will become lifelong friends.

"Come in quick, Dr. Larry. Little girl shot right now."

I run down the slim hallway to where we keep trauma victims. There I recognize the family of three I'd attempted to save. The mother and father are bent over their limp girl. She looks to be about seven. I go to her. Her body is still warm; she has rice in her mouth. There is an entrance wound at the rear of her neck around the seventh cervical vertebra. She has no carotid pulse; her chest does not move. No rise or fall. Her father knows she is dead, but he still expects the American doctor to do something. His eyes plead.

What can I do? How had this happened? I had thought my honking horn had saved them.

Dazed, I swipe her mouth clear of rice with my index finger. Next, I start an IV in her arm. Then pushing on her emaciated thorax, I close my mouth over hers. In and out. In and out I breathe. No oxygen, no blood circulating, no chance. She is dead. But for minutes I cannot stop breathing in and out on her mouth, pushing on her sternum. As a doctor, I know there is not going to be a miracle; yet I'm desperate and pray for one.

The dead girl's father approaches me. *Ah gun*, he says. Thank You. He actually thanks me.

So I give up, back away. "I'm so sorry."

His wife cries without tears. Lifting their little girl into their arms, they leave the hospital, disappearing into the crowded camp.

I look at my watch. It's barely 8 a.m. Damry hands me a towel and I wipe her blood off my hands.

Khmer Rouge Welcoming

The Khmers of Nong Chan had a fateful answer for all the atrocities. When I examined the blind teenager's scarred cornea and asked what happened, the answer was Pol Pot. When I tried to comfort a young woman who had been raped in the forest, the answer was Pol Pot. He had become the very personification of all the evil done to them by the Khmer Rouge.

Reluctantly, I agreed to Hans's invitation. Hans was a Dutch doctor, who, for three months, had been asking me to come and see where he worked. We drove the battered jeep into and around giant potholes, along muddy, narrow roads, until the road and jungle joined. Out of the jeep we began to hike through the forest, the trees dripping as we climbed over huge logs in the steamy wet of June in Cambodia. Where were we going? Hans had been assigned to the Khmer Rouge camp, and I was curious.

The rainy season had at last washed the air clean of torturous dust. It was the hottest season of the year, the humid air so close I felt I was in a steam bath. We crossed ravine after ravine on thin bamboo bridges, maybe 12 inches wide; mostly, I crawled on my hands and knees. As we walked in the tall, wet trees, we watched monkeys that were watching us. Finally, we were greeted by a smiling young woman in the typical Khmer Rouge black pajama-like uniform, accompanied by two solemn teenage boys with AK-47s slung over their shoulders.

Hans and the young people led us to the blue-tarp tent hospital. It was quiet, orderly—none of the chaos that prevailed at our Nong Chan border camp, where entire families slept on connected cots made of bamboo. Some cots had partitions between them, but most patients slept and ate on one continuous platform. The noise was deafening. Outside, every day, hundreds of people waited in the hot sun for food. Children with leprosy, starving children, and—still—mothers who smiled.

At Hans's camp, there were mostly Khmer Rouge soldiers—men and their families. Women and men separated, in huge canvas tents. Sitting, smoking, talking—they appeared so much healthier than the civilians I treated. There were separate cots and a separate surgery, where a dentist took shrapnel and bullets from arms, backs, and heads. It was a war camp, yes, but very different from Nong Chan.

Then it was time. I was brought here to meet Colonel Trang, a Khmer Rouge leader. Not as simple as it sounds. To be a Khmer Rouge leader meant he had to be complicit in the killing of innocent civilians: those who wore glasses, those who spoke French, those who showed any signs of Western influence. I knew this because it was told to me by the survivors, those who ended up in my camp.

I knew, too, that the Russians backed the Vietnamese, and the Chinese backed the Khmer Rouge. But who cared about the ordinary Khmer? Not my own country, certainly, with the policies of Nixon and Kissinger that entrapped Cambodian civilians, stirred the pot, and threw the country into a maze of self-destruction.

We met outside the hospital tent: Colonel Trang, Hans, an interpreter (of sorts), and myself. Between French and English and gestures, we carried on a conversation. The colonel seemed 'well kept'—well fed, shaved, and wearing simple clothes. He was calm. That is what I remember most. As if all the violence he oversaw, the killing he knew was happening as we spoke, was almost incidental. I held myself aloof.

The Colonel asked "Do you have a family?"

"Yes I do."

"How long will you stay in Cambodia?"

"Three months total."

"Thank you for helping my people."

The last sentence sent a chill through me. I was helping those the Khmer Rouge had harmed. It was a kind of compartmentalizing, as if he had no concerns about what was happening all around us. I wanted to scream: What the fuck are you talking about? But I kept my anger in check.

A black-clad youth brought out a little cooler. The Colonel reached in and offered me an Orange Crush. There we stood in the steaming forest, the air calm. He smiled. I smiled. We lifted the cans of Orange Crush, clinked them together, and drank.

I Know Your Heart

The Mekong is the lifeline of Cambodia, just as the Rio Grande is here in New Mexico. The rivers are present and eternally flowing, merging, replenishing. They are life-sustaining, irrigating fields of rice and alfalfa respectively. When I was in Cambodia, along the river's shores children smiled and waved. Lean boys swam and rode water buffaloes in the waters. Beautiful children as children are all over the world.

One morning, coming out of the camp, I got out of my truck. I was covered with sweat, and felt the sweat, the work, the people I had tried to care for—felt them in my bones. The smell of the camp overwhelmed my senses. The odor of death, of cholera, of shit. The smell of the dying. I walked the muddy side of a pond on the Thai-Cambodian border. The water was murky. I pushed my glasses back on my head, cupped my hands and poured the water over my face. I still do this here in New Mexico, after a hike. As I come down and reach a stream crossing, I wash my face in its cold water.

I was in my third and final month working in Nong Chan Camp. I'd been there since March 1980, and now it was June. It was hot and dry, and always dusty. The monsoons would soon begin. In those three months, I had worked all day, seven days a week, in what the Red Cross called a hospital. Nong Chan was a makeshift village of 60,000 refugees. French, Swiss, and British doctors and nurses were also part of the throng.

The camp was a major feeding center for thousands of Khmers who fled the Khmer Rouge and the Vietnamese. On one side of the camp, each day ten UNICEF volunteers fed lines and lines of refugees—fed them bowls of rice and gave out handfuls of seeds for the farmers to go back to Cambodia and plant. But the starving farmers ate the seed and stayed in the camp for safety. On the hospital side of the camp, at the end of the day, there would still be hundreds waiting for medical help. "We'll be back tomorrow," we'd say, looking down at the ground. Lines of people waiting with their sick children, parents who were sick themselves. God, it was a hard thing to see.

We had to leave at night, we were told, for our safety. But, in reality, the Thais didn't want us to witness the killings of Khmers who were trying to escape from Cambodia into Thailand.

In the camp, meanwhile, whole families slept under their open flat wagons, which were covered with blue plastic tarps. Others slept in makeshift tents made from the tarps.

On the first day we arrived, Pierre Perrin, medical director of the International Committee of the Red Cross, spoke to the teams of volunteer doctors who worked at different border camps: the Americans (mine), the Swiss, French, Japanese, Australians, Swedish, Canadians, and British. Each team consisted of one doctor and five nurses. "You all have to decide whether you are a One: If there is active shelling by the Vietnamese or the Khmer Rouge, you want your team to stay; Two: If there is a history of shelling that day, you will be available; or, Three: If there is a chance of shelling and you want to be evacuated." Each doctor was responsible for a team of nurses and one technical assistant—a large responsibility. As I was trying to decide between One and Two, Pierre announced to the entire group: "Except your team, Larry; your team is a Three."

Later, sheepishly, I asked him why we were singled out for 'protection.'

"Larry, if a thousand Khmers die tonight, the world won't give a shit. If I, or say, the French die, it will make the back pages of *Le Monde*. But if you or if an American dies, it will fuck up the entire relief effort."

As I explained earlier, I had left my practice in New Mexico because I wanted to help in Cambodia. I thought I could make a difference. Before leaving the United States, I had stayed at The Hotel Washington in the nation's capital and went out to dinner at the Palm Restaurant with my sister and brother-in-law. They were proud of me and treated me to a three-pound lobster. Suddenly, the enormity of what I was doing, leaving four children and a wife so I could fly to Thailand, sent me into a panic attack. I couldn't eat. I went back to my room, settled down, and went to McDonald's. Ah, a Big Mac. My last one for three months.

Once in Cambodia I was hardly alone in making sacrifices. I will never forget the Australian mother who weaned her own daughter so she could breast feed malnourished Cambodian infants—scores of infants. She would go from one malnourished child to another, offering her milk. She did this until she became so malnourished herself that we had to send her home.

One morning a Cambodian man wearing glasses came into the camp. As far as I knew, glasses had been forbidden by the Khmer Rouge. Glasses were considered a sign of intellectualism, a signal of Western influence, an indication that one had received an education denied to most Khmers—in short a sign of elitism. Damry was a wiry, short man, with dark black hair, full lips, and huge eyes. When speaking English, he hesitated between his words, speaking slowly to be sure he had selected the proper word and was pronouncing it as correctly as he could. English was his third language; he also spoke French. He was one of the gentlest people I'd ever met.

Damry was a godsend. I was in charge of the 'hospital' and needed a translator; Damry fit the bill as best he could. He'd follow me on my rounds, right behind me, learning both medicine and more English. He worked as hard as anyone—harder actually. He worked with me all day long and was left in charge at night.

At night, we (the doctors and nurses) were evacuated by the Thais to a huge field with corrugated cardboard houses. One day when I came back into the camp, I saw fresh blood stains on the bamboo beds. When I'd left the evening before, there were 200 patients. Now there were only a handful. What, I wondered, had happened? History never recorded this. But neither did I. I was so involved with the day-to-day, almost moment-to-moment tragedies that I simply dove into work.

I asked Damry, "What happened?"

Damry said only, "It was a bad night, Dr. Larry."

One morning while making rounds with Damry,

we visited a 38-year-old man who was actively dying. He was coughing blood due probably to untreated tuberculosis. We had no oxygen in this forgotten camp. Gasping for breath, his neck sucking in, his intercostal muscles struggling for air, the man was dying and I could not help him. I asked Damry to tell the patient to "reach out to the Buddha." In retrospect, I remember Damry's puzzled look. Yet out of his respect for me, he obliged.

For years prior to going to Cambodia, I had been part of a group that would turn out to be a cult. The guru, a transported Easterner named Herman Redneck, was simplistic in his approach but powerful in his intentions. When he learned I was going to Cambodia, he instructed me to tell the Khmers to "reach out to the Buddha."

How presumptuous I was. I was only 32, knew no suffering or loss, had no exposure to Buddhism. And here I was, unabashed, telling this dying man who had been a victim of genocide to reach out to the Buddha.

Damry spoke to the patient; the dying man responded. They both looked down.

I tried again, "Damry, tell him to reach out to the Buddha."

The man turned his head and uttered a few words.

"What did he say, Damry?"

Damry paused. "He says he's got diarrhea, Doctor Larry."

I stopped my entreaty.

Another day, a man in his late 40s showed me his rotten tooth, swollen cheek, fetid breath. I grimaced, but next to the seizing child, the typhoid-infected old woman, and the cholera tent overflowing with humanity and excrement, my priorities were clear.

For three days (or was it five?) I kept injecting him with penicillin and morphine. Procrastinating? Finally, and only by his gentle nagging, he prevailed upon me to try to remove the tooth. But how? I'm a doctor, not a dentist (or a jaw smith as we arrogantly called them in medical school). I knew next to nothing about that orifice. For the largest relief effort of the 20th century, you'd think the world could have spared one dentist for the Thai-Cambodian border.

I led the man into the 'treatment' area, a tent made from a tarp full of rips and tears and holes. The bad thing about these holes was that they allowed in the monsoon rains. On the other hand, these holes let in more light—a definite boon in this hospital where there was no electricity.

As I began my first attempt at a tooth extraction, Cora, a nurse originally from Vermont, held a huge flashlight. *How do I numb the man's jaw? Inject above the tooth or block the nerve?*

Feeling the gingival-buccal border where the gum line meets the cheek, I injected Xylocaine with epinephrine. A Swiss doctor loaned me a tooth extractor (think pliers). Slowly, very slowly in a back and forth motion, I tugged at the rotten tooth. The man also had end stage pulmonary tuberculosis (that's what got him into the hospital). Throughout this procedure, he was coughing continuously, and bringing up bloody sputum which covered my bare hands. I had no choice other than to wipe it off on my pants. Fortunately this was before the HIV days.

Using the extractor, I pulled at this man's tooth as he grimaced. *Oh God, what if I break it off and leave the root in place?* Slowly, begrudgingly the tooth loosened, and I was able to get it out. *Did I get the whole thing?* After all these years of training I can only compare it to the teeth I put under my children's pillows. Believe me, this guy's tooth looked nothing like those small pearls.

After I finished, the man looked at his tooth and smiled and brought his palms together, the Buddhist gesture of gratitude. He died ten days later—but not in pain.

———

By June, Damry and I had been working together nonstop for three months. It is difficult for those who have never been in a war zone, especially if you are a civilian, to imagine what our days were like. There were times when the staff would leave the hospital because of nearby shelling; we'd hide behind sandbags, as if that would protect us. There was a pit, dug by the Khmers, which was theoretically safer, but most of the Westerners were afraid of the snakes, me included. The patients would be left in the hospital tent, while refugees hid under wagons or fled into the forest. The noise of shelling is singular—it literally shakes you to your teeth. (I'll never forget the first Fourth of July after I returned home. When the kids set off firecrackers, my whole body twitched.)

On what would be my last day at the hospital there, Damry and I agreed to leave the 'real' world, if only for an hour, and share a lunch together, away from the hospital. We wandered out, walkie-talkie on my shoulder (to alert me, not Damry, about invasions or evacuations). As we walked through the dusty dirt fields, we placed our feet with care to avoid mines. Damry insisted on going first as we approached a two-story watchtower, from which ordinary Khmers could view the forest to see who or what might be coming for them. The forest is also where couples went to make love. One day, two bodies were brought into the hospital on a bamboo stretcher, naked, intertwined. Their legs had been mutilated; they must have lain down together upon a land mine.

Damry and I had brought American food with us that day: two oranges, two Cokes, a tin of tuna, and the Khmer's staple, white rice. We sat in the watchtower and ate with our fingers. It was our longest time together without interruption since we'd first met three months ago. We just sat, eating, observing the sky.

Damry, in his gentle way, said to me: "Dr. Larry, I know your heart."

I choked up with tears. An hour passed and we looked down. Surrounding us were hundreds of people, many smiling. Perhaps they were smiling at our kinship, I thought wishfully, or the quietness of my radio. Whatever had prompted them, they were sharing with us a peaceful moment, isolated in time.

Larry with Ouk Damry, 2004

Michael (Who is like G-d?)

I am waiting. Standing before the entryway for United Airlines. It's June of 1981, a year since I left Cambodia. My three oldest boys are with me: Matthew, Jordan, and Lucas. They are twelve, eight, and seven. It has been months since I heard from the United Nations High Commission on Refugees. I am attempting to adopt Chhoeut NLN.

They'd given us two days notice. We'd received a telex from UN. We should meet Chhoeut at the Albuquerque, New Mexico, airport.

Why this boy? Here was another child, the sixth, coming into our family. Here was the thread to my three-month experience in Cambodia. Here was a link to what was the most intense, potent, oppressive, disaster-filled, transfiguring three months of my life.

We named the child Michael. We thought keeping his name in our small rural community might add more strangeness to this already different child, this stranger. Thinking about it now, I wish we had kept Chhoeut and fostered more Cambodian culture and ideas. Yet he wanted to forget the land where he had lost so much. Somehow, too, the name Michael, which in Hebrew means, 'Who is like G-d?' and asks a question, in some ways reminds me of what I interpreted as a deep spirituality in Michael, some place of worship he entered into privately. As I would quickly learn, he guarded that private space well.

I first met Chhoeut in front of the Catholic Relief Services Hospital in the largest refugee camp in Thailand, Khao-I-Dang. He had lost five brothers and sisters, his father, and his mother. He also survived for four years alone in the jungle. With his open cleft lip and palate he was scorned by his people.

I had gone to Khao-I-Dang because I knew it included 1,200 unaccompanied minors. These were the ones who were known to be truly orphans.

The assurance that a child was truly orphaned had become important in the adoption process because of situations that had developed in the past. All too often when Europeans or Americans had adopted Asian children, their parents would reemerge from the chaos of war to claim their children. So the United Nations wanted to be positive that those children up for adoption truly were orphans—and needed medical help that could not be offered in the camps.

I had heard these stories; but at the time, I was inside the story. Women would come into Nong Chan Camp in Cambodia, and say they had found a child in the forests on the Cambodian side. The pain, the sadness, overwhelmed me. I would take their child and turn her or him over to the UN person. I couldn't sleep after this type of exchange. I thought of my own children and the love and desperation these parents must have had to sacrifice their children so that they might find a better life. We'd send children to Khao-I-Dang in Thailand; but then mothers would come back in one or two days looking for their child. The Thais only let people in who had medical emergencies that we couldn't care for on the border. It was totally confusing.

Some mothers got into the camp, others were turned away. From that point on, we'd keep the children for days in case their parents returned to get them, which they often did.

Because of this experience I wanted to adopt a Khmer child, a child who had medical needs that could not be dealt with in the camps. I'd leave my border camp in Nong Chan to see the children in Khao-I-Dang. The Khmer woman translator told the children, "This doctor is looking to adopt you..." The children swarmed around me, swirls in a pool. I never made that mistake again. I secretly watched the children from a distance, so they would not know my intention and feel disappointment when they were not chosen.

Chhoeut told me through an interpreter that he was 11 years old. Years after his adoption, when we were living in Taos, he asked me, "Why am I so short?"

I explained, "You are young, Asian, and have suffered malnutrition, which might have stunted your growth."

He replied, "Pop, I'm older than you think." It turned out that he had lied to me, shaving two years off his age, thinking that at 13 he'd be too old to adopt. Always the survivor and always competent.

Chhoeut had an innate ability to prosper. In his biography, which he wrote to get into college and which was subsequently published in the *LA Times,* he recalled: "I had to leave the land where Khmer slaughtered Khmer." He had never gone to school in Cambodia. In Taos, he went to Vista Grande and Taos High. In high school, he was an exchange student in Sweden; in college, an exchange student in Ecuador; after college a

Michael and Larry, 1981

Fulbright scholar in New Zealand. Those were the most important things for him. Travel and education.

So here we were in Albuquerque, at New Mexico's largest airport, with its stores, artworks, and carved wooden chairs. Native American artifacts hanging alongside the airlines' schedules. It was a small airport, and in 1981 you could wait right at the gate for your visitors.

Chhoeut arrived. He was the last out of the plane. Alone, skinny and small, a serious and frightened face, he walked down the boarding ramp with a sign around his neck: *My Name Is Chhoeut NLN. My Sponsor in America is Dr. Larry Schreiber.* The sign also included my office phone number. I looked around for an accompanying adult, who would tell me about the long journey. However Chhoeut was alone.

At first I was puzzled. Could they not have spared an adult to accompany this small child? Then puzzlement turned to anger. I felt as if he had been set adrift in a lifeboat, in the middle of an ocean, in a place where he didn't speak the language, didn't know the customs, had no idea what to expect. How dare they! It was only then that I realized NLN was not his last name—it stood for *No Last Name.* I wondered how he had traveled the globe alone—alone, as he had been in Cambodia for four years. Alone was his trademark, then and now. I looked into his eyes and I remembered.

He recognized me. He put his palms together and bowed. I returned the gesture. Then, in my enthusiasm and sympathy, I went to put my arms around him, in the 'American' way. He stiffened. My sons smiled at their new brother.

Later that evening, we arrived at a hotel in Albuquerque before the three-hour trip to San Cristobal. Chhoeut later told me he'd thought we owned the entire hotel, that it was a home. He was shocked when his new brothers dove into the pool the next day. He told me later. "I'd never seen a swimming pool. I only saw people swim in our rivers, or ride water buffaloes."

The Red Sock

Meanwhile back at the office, post-Cambodia, my private practice was moving at a snail's pace. It was so slow some days that I would leave and go to the tennis ranch, where my children swam in a rundown old pool. My nurse, Donna, would beep me if a patient showed up. Eventually, the practice became overwhelmingly busy. I needed a partner. Ellen Warren, M.D., joined me in 1982, and we became Family Practice Associates of Taos.

Practicing medicine in Taos during the '70s and '80s was very different than it is now. For one thing, family practice physicians had to do everything. There were very few specialists. No emergency room doctors, no inpatient hospitalists. I was often called to cover the ER to see unassigned patients who did not have a primary physician—often, tourists traveling through town. I was on call every night, and it wasn't unusual to be up three nights in a row. It was worse than being an intern.

One night, an IV was dislodged from a patient, Sara Louise Hirschberg. She was very New York, even though she was from Pennsylvania. With a lot of class. Like this: She used to go to Santa Fe for dialysis—we didn't have a unit in Taos then—and bring me back a pastrami sandwich each week. That's a New Yorker; it didn't hurt that she was Jewish and knew good pastrami.

Well, now Sara Louise Hirschberg was dying. The nurses couldn't get the IV back in. I was so tired I didn't think I could make it to the hospital. Fortunately Dr. Cetrulo was there. Since he knew Mrs. Hirschberg, he told me to go back to sleep, that he would do the chore. He walked into her room and asked her where she wanted the IV. She replied, in a thick New York accent, "In the patient in the next bed." Sara died four hours later.

Another time, I was called at 4 a.m. to evaluate a teenager in early labor who had no doctor, and to also see a man with chest pains, a tourist, to weigh in on whether he'd had a myocardial infarction, a heart attack. It was what we label a 'soft call.' Nobody really thought he was having a heart attack. They just wanted to be sure.

I had delivered a baby the night before, at 2 a.m., then admitted an alcoholic with a gastrointestinal bleed. I'd worked the entire day, gone home, and was finally, blessedly asleep when the hospital called about the two patients.

Dressing quickly in the near dark, trying not to wake my family, I threw on a winter vest. Preoccupied, thinking of my plan of action for both of my new patients, I slipped on one red sock and somehow could not find the other one. After hopping around trying to find the other sock, I concluded that it was hopelessly lost. So I put on black socks and stuffed the one red sock in the pocket of my winter vest, too tired to put it away.

In those predawn hours, half awake, I traveled to the hospital, which was 17 miles south of my home in San Cristobal. I loved that drive: the occasional elk, the quietness of downtown Taos. At the hospital, I first went to the OB suite to see if the young woman was in active labor. She was in early labor and had a clear-cut rupture of her membranes (water), a clear fluid with cheesy substance (vernix) coming out. I didn't want to do too many pelvic exams on her because of the chance of infection, so I deferred on the exam until she entered more active labor. I reassured the grandmother, who seemed about my age, that everything would be OK. They both looked at me strangely, but I did not care or have time to analyze why.

Next, off to the Emergency Room for the Texas tourist with atypical chest pain. He was in his mid-forties, a smoker, with high cholesterol. Although his pain did not sound cardiac, I felt better admitting him to the hospital, even with a normal EKG, so we could monitor him and get serial EKGs and cardiac enzymes in looking for muscle damage to the heart.

The patient listened intently as I outlined my plan. He was fearful, being far from urban Dallas. He looked at me much the same way the young girl and grandmother had, but seemed to relax as I told him that I just wanted to make sure he wasn't in any imminent danger.

Feeling confident and complete, I headed out of our two-bed emergency room. Just then the Texas heart patient said, "Excuse me, doctor, I think you dropped your red sock."

I turned around slowly and saw my red sock on the emergency room floor. It seemed it was waiting for me to scoop it up. However, it did not fit my self image as the reassuring doctor who was in control of all things medical, so I did what came naturally, I lied.

"That is not my red sock." After all who could prove it?

"But doctor," he retorted, "it matches the one on your shoulder."

I should have replied, "Now where the hell did that come from?" Instead, I just leaned over, picked up the red sock that had fallen from my pocket onto the floor, threw it over my other shoulder, shook hands with the Texan, and wordlessly stumbled out of the room, feeling like a schmuck.

Becoming the AIDS Doctor

didn't choose to become the HIV doctor in Taos. I never learned about AIDS in school. As Sir William Osler said about syphilis, "To know syphilis is to know medicine." The same can be said of AIDS. To know AIDS in the 1980s was to know medicine. I learned about it through my patients.

Joseph Martinez was the first.

I had known him for ten years when he came into my office with his wife, Lori. I had taken care of Mr. Martinez's children, then his grandchildren. He was heterosexual, Hispanic, born in Questa. Now he had horrible headaches and a stiff neck. I'd read about cryptococcal meningitis but never diagnosed it or treated it. All of a sudden, young healthy men were presenting with diseases I'd only read about—diseases that usually affected older and sicker people with damaged immune systems from cancer, from chemotherapy, from congenital immune deficiencies.

I was perplexed. I did a spinal tap and had the lab tech do an 'India-ink prep' on the spinal fluid. She had never done one, and I had never seen one. We both looked at the books and confirmed: The patient had cryptococcal meningitis. We treated him with intravenous antifungals. Along the way, he developed more signs of immunodeficiency. *Pneumocystis carinii pneumonia.* PCP is a severe pneumonia never seen in healthy people.

I realized he must have contracted AIDS because he was a hemophiliac. He had received multiple transfusions of clotting factor 8 over the years, but it only took one infected lot to get him. Mr. Martinez and I talked. "Am I going to die, Dr. Larry? Do I have the gay disease?" I had no test to confirm it; the HIV antibody test wouldn't be discovered until 1985. But he had all the clinical symptoms and the AIDS defining illness.

We had very little in the arsenal to fight with at that time. They discovered AZT in 1987, but it was not very effective when used alone. It wouldn't be until 1996 that we developed highly active antiretroviral therapy. HAART changed the whole landscape, and AIDS was no longer an automatic death sentence.

But here was this man I'd known for years, asking me if he was going to die.

One Thanksgiving, I left my family at the table and traveled with my sons Lucas and Jordan, who were nine and ten at the time, to Mr. Martinez's trailer in Questa. His wife had phoned me. Inside this narrow space, we found him lying on the bed, jaundiced and cachectic (emaciated, with a loss of muscle mass). It was time to go to the hospital.

The Catholic church, led by Father Michael O'Brien, was supportive, and scores of parishioners visited him. Joseph Martinez was the first AIDS patient admitted to Holy Cross Hospital. He was not a homosexual or an IV drug user. It was because of his 'normal profile' that AIDS would become acceptable in the predominantly rural Hispanic and Catholic culture in and around Taos. He paved the way for all AIDS patients who followed. Joseph Martinez died peacefully, with his wife and children by his bedside.

After I'd treated Mr. Martinez, word got out, and I was besieged with men who had AIDS. They were two distinct groups: gay Hispanic males coming home to die, and older gay Anglos coming to Taos with the hope of healing, attracted to the mountain.

Between 1982 and 1996, I had one AIDS patient in the hospital at all times. One patient died every month. It became the leading cause of death for *all* men between the ages of 25 and 44.

In August of 1992, a thin Hispanic boy nervously sat in my office. "I can't see well and I'm losing weight." Examining his retina, I saw he had 'mustard and ketchup' spots, all compatible with cytomegalic virus—a late sign of AIDS, which could cause blindness. On his tongue, he had grooves, which made me think of oral hairy leukoplakia. On his mouth and throat were white plaques, which indicated a yeast infection. On his back, on one side, he had painful blisters. He had shingles. There was a medical textbook in this one frightened boy. His blood tests came back HIV positive, with a CD 4 count of 15. His viral load was over 500,000. All of these numbers meant his immune system was devastated.

"Son, you have AIDS. We will fight it together. First, you need ganciclovir IV to save your sight."

He was shaking, a terror that makes it impossible to listen. It was a feeling that I grew to learn too well. The young man had just come out as gay. I couldn't say, "You have six months to live." I just couldn't. He had too much to deal with first.

"Please have your partner come in," I said.

He nodded. A few months later, his partner lost him.

Another time, Jim, an Anglo gay man, lay dying at home. He had no partner and so, one sunny Sunday afternoon, I visited him in his home in Ranchos de Taos. He was at the end, covered with blotches from Kaposi's sarcoma, the *gay man's cancer,* thin as a rail, confused by multifocal leukoencephalopathy, an inflammation of the brain. Jim was afraid. Yet he couldn't convey his thoughts. I lay down next to him, and stroked his forehead. I told him, "Everything will be alright." He died a few minutes later.

How did I feel treating AIDS patients, especially before the drugs that removed the death sentence? I was afraid whenever I was drawing blood or suturing and, like so many others, I felt numbed by the numbers of people I saw die. And yet I felt intellectually stimulated. Here was a disease that I as a doctor could find out how to fight. A disease not known in my medical school years. It was hard, very hard, but there is nothing like seeing others' phobic responses to clarify for oneself where one stands.

The "Good Doctor"

Before leaving my doctoring stories and moving on to my family and kids, let me share one last memory, which demonstrates how the good, the bad, and the ugly can manifest in the world of medicine.

Prior to my 1976 arrival in Taos, the town's only OB/GYN—let's call him Doctor Number 1—had shot a bullet through his temporal lobe playing West Texas Russian Roulette.

The next OB/GYN, Doctor Number 2, was an elderly man, also from Texas, who was mechanically blessed but whose ethics were fogged by the bottle and inherent prejudice, particularly when he railed against 'fucking hippies' before his own ethanol level fell below the legal intoxication limit.

OB/GYN Doctor Number 3 was discovered to be a registered arms dealer.

After a while, I wondered if Taos was better off with our town's old general practitioner/surgeon, Dr. Al Rosen.

By the time I arrived in Taos, Rosen had delivered thousands of Taoseños, as evidenced by the slew of kids named Albert or Alberto. Whenever I needed a C-section, he always came to the hospital dressed only in a bathrobe over his underwear, a cigar hanging from his mouth. He knew everyone but remembered no one's name. After removing his bathrobe and donning his scrubs, he'd C-section a baby out in three minutes, tell us to close, change his scrubs, slip on the bathrobe, inhale his cigar, and be off like Zorro.

Dr. Rosen also had a very steep daredevil ski run named for him. He continued to ski to his dying day, even when he finally had to strap an oxygen tank to his back.

Given the luck Taos had with the three previous gynecologists, we were delighted when Dr. Munn arrived in 1986. She was young, board certified, dressed appropriately, and looked and acted "normal." Women were glad to have a woman as their OB/GYN.

At first there were some disturbing rumors, a few complaints from patients, but nothing too dramatic. We were so happy to have this knowledgeable, energetic doctor that we didn't pay attention. But rumors persisted.

Finally, a situation developed at Holy Cross Hospital that could not be ignored. Dr. Munn had been sending Pap smears to an outside lab. Our hospital's pathology reports indicated "normal organs" from a fair amount of her surgeries. When we questioned her, she told us that her Pap smears from the lab she chose showed early cancer or severe dysplasia, a precancerous condition. So we let it go.

Nevertheless, when normal pathology kept resurfacing on patients whose uterus, cervix or ovaries were removed, we grew alarmed. We ordered and obtained Dr. Munn's pathology reports. They proved she was doing unnecessary surgeries. She had lied. She was putting Taos women at risk—for no medical reason. So what reason was there?

Finally, though I don't remember how, the state attorney general's office in Santa Fe got involved. This wasn't a civil malpractice issue but an issue of criminal behavior. Malpractice is a judgment error: a person comes in with chest pains, the doctor on duty thinks it's muscular and sends him home, where he drops dead. A criminal action is an intended act of harm.

A Mr. Singh, from the attorney general's office, phoned me. I was glad to get the call. I wanted this out in the open. Mr. Singh told me that the AG's office was bringing a number of charges against the "good doctor." But he only wanted me as a witness to one particular case.

He asked me to review the chart of a 47-year-old patient of mine. She had menorrhagia, heavy pathological periods to the point of profound anemia. I had treated her conservatively. First I prescribed hormones, then I transfused her with red blood cells, and finally I completed a dilation and curettage of her uterine lining. The D&C was done in the operating room so we could stop her pathological bleeding. But in this case, we failed. Therefore, I called Dr. Munn, who performed a hysterectomy and saved the woman's life.

Given that the appropriate procedures Dr. Munn had followed, and the success of the treatment in this case, I couldn't understand why the AG's office would want to bring up this particular case. Over the phone, I asked him: "Mr. Singh, why in God's name are you reviewing this particular case? This is one of the few cases where she was right!"

"How large was your D&C patient's uterus?" Singh asked.

We size uteri according to how large they are when distended by a fetus from 4-40 weeks. "Six weeks size," I answered.

"Are you sure?"

"Yes. I ordered an ultrasound that accurately reports the size. Plus, I had sounded the uterus in the operating room, putting a metal rod through the cervical opening until it hit the top of the uterus. But what's the point? Dr. Munn did a good job in this case and saved the lady's life."

"Don't you get it, Dr. Schreiber?" he replied. "She lied when she did not have to lie. She said the uterus was 18 weeks in size. She is a sociopath and a pathological liar, and her attorneys want a plea bargain—for her to go back and do another year of residency. She will never be a good doctor. She has the technical skill but no conscience! We want to protect patients from her in the future."

"You're right," I said.

"So, will you testify?"

"Gladly."

Three days later, the expected call came from Dr. Munn's lawyer. He had a thick East Coast accent, either New York or Jersey, and spoke so quickly that I could barely understand him. I had been out of New York for too long.

"Did you consult Dr. Munn about a 47-year-old patient with menorrhagia and life-threatening anemia?"

"Yes," I said.

"Did the patient need a hysterectomy?"

"Yes."

"Did Dr. Munn do a good job?'

"Yes, she did."

"Fine. Then we will pay your fee."

He told me the fee was $500—I would have done it for free.

It was a long drive to the hearing room in Albuquerque. There I met her lawyer, a little shrimp of a man with a suit he could not button, because of his abdominal girth, and a familiar arrogance about him. He asked me the same questions before the judge came in, and I accepted check #1142 payable to me signed by Dr. Munn. She (the good doctor) was dressed in a blue tailored suit, yellow blouse, and brown high heels. She smiled at me.

The judge entered. He was about 60, with receding hair and a strong, quiet voice. He called me as the first witness. The defense lawyer asked the prepared expected questions:

"Did you consult Dr. Munn?"

"Yes."

"Did the patient need a hysterectomy?"

"Yes."

"Did Dr. Munn complete the operation successfully?"

"Yes."

"No more questions, Your Honor."

Next I was questioned by the lawyer from the attorney general's office:

"How large was the uterus?" Mr. Singh asked.

"Six weeks size."

"Are you sure?"

"Yes." I explained how we size uteri.

"Then why do you think Dr. Munn said it was 18 weeks?"

I looked across the small hearing room at this sociopath with good hands but no moral compass. She smiled almost seductively.

"Because she is a liar, sir!" I said.

Her attorney jumped out of his seat objecting loudly as if we were on TV. The judge ordered him to sit down or he would be held in contempt. Mr. Singh stood fast on his position, explaining that my statement was based on fact. Her attorney persisted, but Mr. Singh made sure my comments stayed on the record. In the middle of the argument my eyes locked with the defendant's. She mouthed "fuck you" at me.

Finally, the judge restored order. "OK, Doctor you can go."

I sighed with relief. Light-headed, sweating, my heart beating rapidly, I walked to the "door" of the courtroom and pulled at the knob, but it would not budge. I tried again—no deal. I stood there blinking, befuddled. The judge and the defense lawyer were arguing another point. Finally the judge noticed me standing there and blurted, "Doctor, that's the closet."

Epilogue: The outcome of the trial was that Dr. Munn was told to do another year of residency. She's now making probably $300,000 a year taking out uteri in a nearby state.

Epilogue 2: Recently, 26 years after my last meeting with the good doctor, I received a call from her new attorney. Dr. Munn was being sued. The lawyer heard I'd testified in the past. Obviously, the good doctor had lost her memory as well as her ethics, since her lawyer was asking me to testify on her behalf! I told him the whole story and he thanked me. "Your services will not be needed."

Sometimes It's Just a Smile
(Gina's World)

landed at the airport on the outskirts of Calcutta in July of 1986. The heat! Like someone smothering me. Like trying to speak with a blanket over my face. The colors are overwhelming: a million-hued kaleido-scope of cobalt blue, blood red, saffron yellow, Day-Glo orange, purple, bright greens, glorious magenta—every color of the rainbow plus thousands more yet to be invented. And the mass of people! Most of them were holding signs: cabs for hire; limousines, luxurious and cheap. A moving mass holding their children up, beg-ging, pinching, hustling.

"You want a ride mister?" A man asked.

"Yes," I said and told him where I needed to go.

"Oh, orphanage? Mother Teresa's?"

"No. International Mission of Hope."

"You mean Mother Teresa's. I take you there."

"No. International Mission of Hope—Asha Kendra!"

I entered the sweltering cab, which lurched through a potholed road filled with tuk tuks (motor cycles with carriage) and rickshaws drawn by men, barefoot and skinny, spitting blood. On the cement, spitting out blood. TB. My taxi driver screamed epithets whose words I don't understand but whose meaning is clear: "Get the fuck off the road!"

Before we got to the hotel, the cab started smoking and broke down. "No problem," said the Sikh driver as he lifted up the hood. After a few minutes of magic that included some kind of part change, we were back on our way. As we continued on to the hotel, I began to notice the terrible pollution. In a week, I would be blowing black mucus out of my nose.

We arrived at the Fairlawn Hotel, Calcutta luxury, where the daily rate of $15 included two British meals. The hotel was my anchor in Calcutta. And I needed an anchor, believe me.

Here's what was beautiful to me: The streets were full of people who lived on the sidewalks, sleeping in sleeping bags, blankets, or cardboard coverings. But when the sun rose, they too rose, the way we do at a football game, in a wave. Black-haired children with huge pools for eyes, saris in red, orange, blues. The city turns on the fire hydrants, and the people wash themselves, brush their teeth, pick the nits out of each other's hair. Then, almost on schedule, almost like suburbanites, they leave their 'spots' on the pavement and go to work—hustling, begging, pleading, surviving. At night, they come back to their 'home,' and the air rings with the sound of clarinets, flutes, drums; of people talking, singing, making love, defecating—living.

There were times when I wanted to live and work in Calcutta forever. There was such need, such openness. I never felt threatened. I'd walk all over in the evenings and was always met by kindness, a wave of friendliness. Of course, there were always the hustlers. A short man with a scraggly beard came up to me one evening. Barefoot, wearing loose fabric tied with rope, two sizes too big, he asked: "You want a girl, sir?" I shook my head. "You want a boy?" I walked away.

I had come to Calcutta to adopt Gina. She was reported to be nine years old, but no one knew for sure; the children's histories were hidden and forgotten. I first saw Gina in a photo. I already had eight children, five of whom were adopted. The 'special-needs adoption agencies' had us on their list, sending us magazine after magazine with photos of waiting children. The photo of Gina got to me. She was standing on a chair, holding onto the back, her knees hyperextended. Her right leg was in an awkward position, the foot inverted because the muscles couldn't hold it out—clearly the result of polio.

I had seen hundreds of photos of children, all beautiful, all with some kind of hurt, some kind of disease, showing signs of malnourishment. But Gina stood out. It was her smile, a smile that took up her whole face, as if it were somehow lit from inside. Her black hair flowed past her shoulders, and her dress with its white collar was covered with green and red flowers. She was barefoot, her feet unable to fit into shoes.

So, off to Calcutta I had gone.

At the Fairlawn Hotel, I couldn't help thinking about the opening paragraph of a *Tale of Two Cities*, by Charles Dickens. It describes Calcutta to a tee: "It was the best of times, it was the worst of times, it was the age of wisdom, it was the age of foolishness, it was the epoch of belief, it was the epoch of incredulity, it was the season of light, it was the season of darkness, it was the spring of hope, it was the season of despair..."

After registering at the hotel, I set off for the International Mission of Hope (IMH) to visit with Sherri, a Denver nurse who had married Sunil, a Bengali. After moving to India, she hired an Indian neonatologist who went to hospitals where Indian women underwent abortions.

Since ultrasounds were not routinely performed before abortions, the size and dates of the fetuses were often unknown. Some of the aborted fetuses, in the womb for at least six months, lived and came out crying, so the physician brought them to IMH. About 50 percent of the aborted children survived and were adopted. Some of these survivors would be my plane ticket home.

Gina and I hit it off right away. She spoke a bit of English, enough that with sign language and smiles, we could communicate. From the first, we understood each other. "Ami apanake aneka bhalobasi," she told me in Bengali: I love you very much. This was after four days together, and the words came out easily for me, too. For months before meeting her, I had been looking at Gina's photos, so my heart was already open to her. Later, we always repeated this Bengali phrase to each other, coming and going.

One day, I took Gina and some of her friends to a movie. Now this sounds like a simple, everyday kind of task, doesn't it? At home we would buckle the kids in the cars, put on the air conditioner, drive to the theater, buy popcorn, and wait for the coming attractions. In Calcutta, accompanied by 15 children and Chitra, an adult who worked for the IMH, we grabbed a cab and sat three deep on top of each other, without seatbelts.

At the theater, we sat in the balcony, which shook whenever the kids jumped up and down, as most of them did. Gina was so happy that she sprang up on her chair, laughing. The Bollywood movie was in Hindi, simplistic and punctuated with English dialogue. Chitra sat next to me, repeating the English as if she were translating it. When the actress said, "I love you," Chitra said, "The actress said, 'I love you.'" The film included dancing, singing, and lots of bright colors.

The raucous atmosphere of the movie house stood in marked contrast to a Bengali play I had attended the night before, a dramatic production that moved me, even without my understanding a word. That theater was filled with middle-class Bengali women in beautifully woven saris and men in long dress shirts without collars.

I went to the orphanage every day to see Gina so she would become familiar with me, her new father. I learned that her birth mother still loved her, but having six girls, and the youngest with polio, she knew she could not care for Gina. So she had taken Gina to the orphanage but continued visiting her there. Gina told me that her mother "showed much affection," during her visits. This was not typical.

Around day six, I asked to take Gina with me for an overnight stay. We ate dinner in the Fairlawn Hotel's 'British' dining room, Gina wearing her only dress. The rat that ran across the floor raised nary a peep from the mostly European crowd. A U.S. evangelical group peered at Gina, then at me, and then at the two of us together. Perhaps they hoped I'd baptize Gina. I remember thinking they all had too many teeth.

After dinner, we returned to our room. Gina's legs were callused from crawling on the hot, dusty roadways. She was able to make me understand that she wanted to bathe and needed a bucket. After saying OK, I was able to find one in the closet. The bathtub looked stately with it's claw feet. I left the bathroom to give Gina her privacy and sat on the bed, trying to imagine what her life would be in San Cristobal. What could I offer her? Would she fit in? Was I doing the right thing?

Suddenly, I noticed water seeping from beneath the bathroom door. "Gina!" I yelled. "Are you alright?" No reply.

I pushed open the door and found Gina in her underwear, standing next to the tub, filling the bucket with water from the running bath and pouring it over herself, bathing as she had on the streets of Calcutta. She was smiling, feeling very much at home.

Gina in Fairlawn Hotel in Calcutta

At the hotel, in between times with Gina, I met an Irishman named Sam O'Reilly, whose wife had recently died. As a result, Sam decided to spend a year volunteering at Mother Teresa's Hospice in Kalighat. After we got to know each other somewhat, he invited me to accompany him there.

The day of my visit, we hopped on a bus jammed with what seemed to be hundreds of people. The bus was like an open trolley car, with people hanging on outside, standing in the doorways, and holding onto the windows. Many sat on the roof, with their pots, pans, burlap bags, and children—all hanging on for dear life.

Sam and I pushed our way through the almost impassable slam of people. He held onto me by my belt, so I wouldn't be pushed off the bus at the various stops. Even so, at one juncture, I went tumbling out with a gush of exiting passengers. As the bus started up again, the driver was oblivious to the fact that I was only half on the step, my left leg dragging on the concrete. Luckily, Sam was able to pull me in as the bus roared off toward its next stop.

Mercifully, we reached our destination in Kalighat in safety. Sam clapped me on the back as I resisted the urge to kiss the earth. I had imagined that since Mother Teresa had received the Nobel Prize, her hospice would have labs, donated glucometers, hemoglobin indicators, and chemistry analyzers. But no. Not at all. Inside the building, a former Hindu temple to the goddess Kali, cots were lined up a foot apart, each occupied by a dying person. Family members sat with moaning patients.

I told Sam that I was just here to observe. He nodded and went off to complete his chores. Even here, the smells of Calcutta's trash, smoke and pollution burned my nose, even though the hospice was scrubbed daily. I saw Sam with a small bowl and a spoon, feeding an old man with withered skin, thin as a broomstick. Sam gently offered dal bhat with rice, smiling as he did.

Mother Teresa was in Cuba at the time of my visit, so Sister Luke was in charge. Sam had told her I was an American doctor.

"Oh, you are a doctor?" Sister Luke asked politely. "We have no doctors today. Would you help out?"

I was amazed that this facility, the legacy of Mother Teresa, the Nobel laureate, could ever go a day without a doctor. I rolled up my sleeves, literally, and wound up working for 12 hours.

By this time, July 1986, I'm no stranger to Third World medicine. Cambodia had been my university in dealing with the brutal and bare minimum of conditions. Nonetheless, the work in the hospice is, for me, worse than Cambodia. Here in Calcutta, there is no war, no famine. Just baseline poverty and disease. Deep. Grinding.

I knelt before the different cots with a translator and asked, "What can I do to help you? Are you in pain? Do you have fever or chills?" I gave them drugs, labeled in French, or Russian, sometimes in English. I pushed penicillin, metronidazole, and of course, morphine. Of the 20 or 30 people I treated that day, three died. Peacefully, I hoped.

Four days later, I was approached by Dr. Koshi. He was the very polite and dedicated IMH neonatologist responsible for saving the fetuses that survived abortions.

"Are you a specialist?" he asked.

"No, I'm a family physician."

"Really?"

Dr. Koshi couldn't believe that with all the opportunities in America, I hadn't chosen a more academic—and highly paid—specialty. He asked if I would like to go on rounds with him at the Calcutta Medical College.

"Sure, I'd love to," I replied. Somehow this seemed like the perfect combination, helping out as a doctor while adopting a new daughter.

Calcutta National Medical College is located on 32 Gorachand Road. It is a large building with a portico across the front. Entrance to the building is gained by climbing what seems to be several hundred steps, which are lined with beautiful cloths and rugs laid out for viewing by their sellers. Above the huge door that day (and maybe most days), laundry dropped down over the balcony, adding color to the dull gray of this enormous building.

Once inside, Dr. Koshi joined a group of other white-jacketed doctors, all with fresh haircuts, all standing very straight, all speaking British English, all very much like something out of a colonial-era film. There seemed to be a contradiction, a discontinuity between their perfection in form and manner, their focus on academics, and the mass of people waiting in line to see them.

As I watched this incongruous spectacle, I felt oddly like Nero, fiddling while he watched Rome burn. Here was a group of residents and interns spending their time discussing oncotic pressure in the hypoalbuminemic state of portal hypertension, while the crying needy were screaming in pain, a crew of nurses and surgical assistants treating fractures. The patients moaned with inadequate anesthesia.

It was not my favorite day, and I longed to see little Gina.

After ten days in Calcutta, it was time to bring Gina home. Since I didn't have much disposable income, the IMH agreed to pay my airfare. But they had a condition: Along with Gina, could I also bring home ten infants who were being adopted by other U.S. families?

"Ten?" I replied. "That's a lot to handle."

"You'll have help. And the other infants are only going as far as Seattle."

"Okay, let's do it!"

Accompanied by two Indian adults, I arrived at the airport carrying two baskets with two infants each, plus 40-pound Gina resting on my hip. The other adults carried three infants each. Now, I'm usually an airport neurotic. I like to be at the gate at least one hour before departure, so I can calmly read my *New York Times* and not be anxious about the flight. Not this time. I'm in Calcutta responsible for ten infants, Gina, and two Indian adults. Fourteen visas! Fourteen passports! In those pre-911 days, we all arrived at the gate, panting and sweating, five minutes before the flight took off.

Once airborne, the mostly Indian passengers paid little attention to us. After landing in Bangkok, we put ten infants and one of the Indian adults in one room at the Bangkok Airport Hotel. Gina stayed on a cot in my room.

The next day, late again, we wound up running to the gate, sweating profusely, just making it aboard the Royal Thai airliner. This plane was full of European and American tourists. At first, they thought the babies were 'oh so cute.' A number of the women asked to hold one or the other little darling. "Fine," I thought to myself. "Hold them as long as you want!"

Their attraction lasted all of thirty minutes at the start of the flight. Then they ordered their wine, drank a couple of glasses, reclined their seats, put on eye masks, and drifted back to their world. Meanwhile...

All my good intentions flew out the window. The babies were screaming. I tried to keep their bottles, labeled with each of their names, separate. I kneeled in the aisle, trying to change the diaper of one infant, while one of the Indian attendants tried to find the bottle of another. By the time we reached Seattle, the bottles, the babies, the diapers, were interchangeable. One baby had poop running down his legs; I lifted him with both my hands and held him as far away from my body as possible as I ran down the aisle to the bathroom. The tired passengers on the flight were not amused with our commandeering almost the entire free space on the plane. Throughout this chaos, however, Gina was a marvel, playing with the babies on the floor, smiling and unflappable.

When the trip began, I had looked forward to meeting all the parents who would be waiting for their new babies. But by the time we unloaded in Seattle, I was exhausted and anxious for a moment's peace. So I rushed off the plane, heartened to see the sign *U.S. Residents This Way.* The babies—all of them in baskets—were taken by the Indian assistants in the direction of the other sign: Nonresidents This Way. I slipped through the turnstile with Gina in my arms, and we boarded the next plane. We slept the entire flight from Seattle to Albuquerque.

When we arrived at the Sunport Airport, all my children and Carol were there waiting for their new sister. As we came off the plane and headed for our family, Gina was in my arms babbling in fragmented English and Bengali.

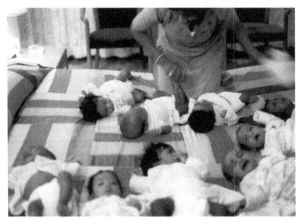

The ten babies

The Children and Me

I did not plan to adopt ten children, let alone wind up with 14. It just happened, like waking up one day and realizing you're old and saying: how did that happen? I am, however, happy with my decisions—or perhaps I should say my fate. The 14 kids have given me the most joy and most grief in my life, a kind of heightened parenting where the lows are much lower but the highs are MUCH higher. I am just as proud of my physician child and my attorney kids as I am of the one who holds a minimum-wage job to support her two children. I won't tell you about all of them but will give you a snapshot of what the days were like.

I was in between marriages in 1991 and had shared custody of the kids. By this time, Michael (from Cambodia) and Matthew (the eldest child) were out of the house. That left me responsible for a brood of 11. I had to be at Holy Cross Hospital by 8 a.m. to make rounds, which on the surface doesn't sound like much, right?

However, I never got to take the quickest, most direct route. There was the stop at Trudy's Discovery House to drop off Reyno for preschool. This was followed by stops at Taos Elementary to leave Lorena and Ciela, at Enos Garcia Middle School for YoRi and Gina, at junior high for Gabrielle, and, finally, Taos High School for Jordan, Mary, Kevin, Lucas and Champa!

People asked if I thought my kids would become doctors, since they were so close to me. I thought they were more likely to become janitors, since having been dropped off early at their schools, they spent so much early-morning time with the custodial staff. Fortunately, Jordan received his driver's license early and did a fair share of the driving, this at a slightly more 'normal' hour.

Actually, these years were delightful. I especially loved picking up the kids. They yelled and talked all the way home—and although hassled and exhausted by the time I made it there, I thoroughly enjoyed it. On the days I wasn't on call, I'd leave the office early, to get home to be with the kids or attend one of their events. There were Reyno's Little League games; ballet lessons for Gabrielle and YoRi; the boys' and girls' soccer games; Taekwondo for Jordan, Gina, Lucas and Kevin; track meets for Mary; and watching Ciela tumble from standing on the shoulders of larger girls at cheerleading practice. Finally there was Lorena's singing with the Mariachi band.

As much as possible, I established a routine that allowed me to be with each of the children separately. Sometimes I would take one or two up the north road above the San Cristobal Valley, on the route to Lama. I would drive along, stopping occasionally at an overlook from which we could see our house. We'd get out of the car—the signal for talk. "I have a crush on Tony," Gabrielle confided. "Pop, I'm the only girl on the boy's soccer team!" Mary boasted.

I always felt relaxed when I was in the mountains with the children. I'd look down on the 'homestead' and feel content. I had done something good and important, given life and this place to these children. It was so different from the city and suburban life that I had known as a child. Here the children could grow up free to roam and play amid enormous beauty. They had least had that option.

At home, without TV reception, we watched movies on a VCR, all on top of each other in the playroom, eating popcorn. Jordan and Lucas demanded quiet; Mary, always vociferous, would punch Kevin, and when I'd call her on it, she'd take off on Rowdy, our bay horse, and disappear for hours.

At that time, we had Rowdy, two goats (Joy and Goaty), four dogs (Autumn, Midnight, Obi, and Shana, who had been shot by an irate neighbor protecting his sheep, so she had only three legs), one cat (Chocolate), one donkey (Isabelle), one sheep (Sheepish), one pig (Piggish), ten chickens, and a slew of rabbits. We were very original with names. Oh, and two highly aggressive geese. We got rid of the geese when they started attacking the children.

When the goats were born, their mother died birthing them. Jordan and Lucas kept the little goats in the bathtub, set their alarm every four hours during the night, and fed the goats milk through a Pepsi Cola bottle and nipple. They kept those little 'kids' alive, and the kids grew up and survived.

By this time, our family was 7.5% of the population of our village of San Cristobal (not including the animals.)

One time, we decided to go camping at Latir Lakes, up near the Colorado border. From the campground, we would then take a long hike with Isabelle the donkey carrying all our goods. However, try as I might, I couldn't get Isabelle into my 1976 Chevy pickup.

So we changed plans and decided to go into the mountains of San Cristobal. After loading the donkey up with saddlebags, we led her to the southern portion of our property, where we tried to get her to go over the bridge. Isabelle refused to budge. So, Lucas and Jordan became the donkey, while Isabelle wandered about the field unencumbered.

Dinner was loud and boisterous, with everyone trying to be heard over everyone else. Juana Lucero from Chihuahua, Mexico worked for me, cooking and caring for my small army. Almost every night at our huge rectangular dining room table, we ate burritos and tacos with lots of rice and beans, the children on tall chairs and booster seats.

As the proud patriarch, I would ask them about school: "Tell me one thing you learned today." Answers came back like, "New Mexico became a state in 1912," "The Native Americans were here first," "I can't remember," "I didn't learn anything today," "Pop, I hate school."

One time, Mary said that Taos was the only place where she was considered an Anglo. Being African-American, she was not one of the three prevailing cultures here. But rather than being looked at as exotic, she was placed in the same category as non-Hispanic or non-Native peoples. Mary felt fine with it, though. Taos was a place that welcomed my private United Nations.

Personally, I found it cool and wonderful to have so many kids from such a diversity of nationalities: Korean, Cambodian, African-American, East Indian, Hispanic, and Anglo—a little world under one roof.

Larry and kids, Taos, New Mexico 1991

I felt satisfied that I had my priorities straight. And no matter what else I did or didn't do in life, this family made it all worthwhile.

And it would soon become even more blissful.

Enter Cathy

n early 1992, I was making yet another attempt to feel like I really belonged in Northern New Mexico. Unfortunately, I was (am) linguistically challenged. No matter how loud or often I spoke Spanish, I didn't quite blend. So I enrolled in Laverne Baily's Spanish One course at the Harwood Library, a part of the University of New Mexico–Taos. This was the third time I had taken Spanish One.

In the class, Ms. Baily asked us personal questions: "¿Estas casado?" "¿Tienes hijos?" "¿Cual es su ocupacíon?"

The most important question to me was the first: Are you married? The beautiful woman across the table from me responded, "Estoy divorciado." *That* I understood. Although she looked very young, she was old enough to be divorced.

In my feeble Spanish, I said, "Estoy divorciado tambien."

Sometimes you just know about your feeling toward someone. Even a stranger. Here was a face to launch a thousand ships. Yeah, I know. But that's exactly how corny my thoughts were. Her face, her expressive amber-brown eyes, the white teeth, a smile to die for, the deep intelligence gleaming from her visage. Her face shook me to my roots. Yeah, I know.

That evening, I was dressed all in black. I wasn't trying to be mysterious—everything else was in the laundry. But after seeing her, I suddenly felt mysterious. I wanted to know her name, so I leaned over her chair as she was writing a check on the table. Printed on the check was a name I recognized. In this small town, even when you don't know the person, you know a lot of facts about them. Cathy Strisik was a teacher for the dyslexic, with a fine reputation at the Taos Valley School—and she was a gifted poet. She had married a Taos artist but was now *divorciado*. What I didn't know was her phone number. How was I going to find out?

Too shy to ask her in class, at home I looked her up in the phone book. No luck. I called information. No luck. So, abandoning my ethics, I went to my office chart, figuring everybody in the county has been to my office at least once. I located her chart and discovered she'd been to my office only once. But once was all I needed to find out her phone number.

The next day, I mustered up the courage to call. I hadn't asked many women out on dates in the last 25 years. A Beefeater's gin made it easier.

After exchanging pleasantries, I dove right in.

"So, Cathy, do you want to go out for a drink after Spanish class?"

"I don't drink."

"How about coffee?"

"I don't drink coffee."

Way to go Larry! I sipped my gin and thought: Boy, I lost this one, so why not go for the bleachers.

"Well, do you want to go out with me?"

"Sure."

Way to go Larry!

After our next Spanish class, we walked together to my Suburban, which was parked in the dirt. I had to boost Cathy up so she could reach the front seat. After helping her into the vehicle, I went around to the driver's side. I was nervous and belched outside the car. When I got inside, Cathy asked, "What is that smell?"

I realized she would never let me get away from the truth.

She smiled and I was smitten again.

We went to the Taos Inn where I had (another) Beefeater. She drank mineral water and had a salad. We talked. And talked. For hours. We talked about people we knew in common, Spanish class, and how long we had lived in Taos and what we loved about this quirky town. I cursed a lot. Later, she told me she found it refreshing. Cathy already knew some things about me: 13 children, physician, co-founder of Child-Rite. She'd also seen me once in the gym in an aerobics class, spastic. Oh well.

Soon thereafter, I took Cathy to my home, where seven of my children were spread out in beds all over the house. The three youngest slept together in the playroom, each in their own small bed with animal headboards. For me, my large family gave me bragging rights. I had dated two women since my divorce, and both were overly exuberant about the children. Cathy was honest—and reserved. Having 13 children was not on her radar.

I fell in love with Cathy before she fell in love with me. It wasn't until six months after our first date that she told me: "I'm in love with you." We were in Ottawa, Canada, because I was president of the North

American Council on Adoptable Children. The council was a 50,000-member advocacy group composed of parents and social workers pushing to free the children held in foster care. I thought: Here I am without the children, away from my office, no doctor trappings. And she loves me!

Her parents were aghast. Here she was with a man 11 years older, with 13 children of many nationalities, a man who was of a different faith, living in a large house in a rural part of Northern New Mexico. *Has our daughter lost her mind?*

They came to visit. I always did well with the parents of girlfriends, I assured myself. I was charming, witty, loud and engaging. I was certain I would win them over. We went to the fanciest, most expensive restaurant in the county, Villa Fontana. I picked up the check, but that wasn't hard. The proprietor, Carlo Gislimberti, had heart disease and no insurance. We bartered.

Cathy's sophisticated New England parents seemed to have had a good time. The next day, however, when they were alone with Cathy, they expressed their displeasure and disappointment.

"He lives in a hippie house!" her mother said.

"He's old!" her father added.

"Well, I'm in love with him," Cathy replied.

After a while, her parents resigned themselves to fate. They loved their daughter and knew she was smart. They would eventually grow to like me, too.

I took Cathy on my motorcycle to a special place overlooking the San Cristobal Valley, where she could see her future home. We looked down over the valley, and I, like some Clark Gable, said, "All this can be yours!"

I know she thought it was one of the schlockiest semi-proposals ever. But I was determined.

"Will you move in with me?" I said.

"I'll think about it," she said.

Seven months later, she did. With one proviso.

"I need a place to write my poetry, and be alone," she said. A reasonable request, considering the children and me. So we had a contractor build a log cabin on the south side of the pond, near a stream. Her sanctuary is still there today. A place she frequents, a place into which I've been invited a grand total of 17 times in 22 years.

Cathy wanted to have a baby. She'd tried with her first husband without success. She had a complete infertility workup, and they found no organic reason for her not to get pregnant. Her ex had fathered a child before and after their marriage.

"Do you want to have a child with me?" she asked.

I replied, "If you can step-parent these 13 kids, I can handle one more."

But I had my own provision. At my age I would not get up to feed the baby after midnight. I felt guilty about it, since I had always shared the nighttime duty taking care of the infants. On the other hand, I was still getting up at night on call, going to the hospital. I needed my rest.

Cathy agreed. Yet, the first night we came home from the hospital, our new baby, Dimitra, cried and cried and cried. I stayed up with her for hours—I couldn't help myself. Cathy slept on. When she woke, she found me holding the baby and felt joyous.

"I think I ruined your life," she said, and we both laughed.

But before I proceed further, let me rewind. Before Dimitra was born, we had tried—unsuccessfully—for eight months to get pregnant. I told Cathy, "We should check my sperm—just to be sure." It had been 14 years since I had impregnated anyone!

Cathy at the time was still living in her apartment above the Harwood Library. So one morning, I drove to her apartment with a carful of kids to take to school. The pathology lab had wanted a fresh semen sample. I said to the kids packed inside, "Gina, Gabrielle, Kevin, Lorena, Ciela, Reynaldo and YoRi: I have to visit Cathy for a minute." A New York minute.

I raced up her steps, and 'collected' a sample with Cathy's assistance. Okay, it was five minutes. I raced downstairs with my specimen in a urine container, and drove off to four schools and left the innocents at the doors of their various schools with no one, I thought, the wiser. When I reached the lab, I had to enter a patient's name on the requisition form. I didn't want my name on it, since all the lab workers knew me, and my situation. So I named the 'patient' Hymie Samaras, combining both our heritages, Jewish and Greek, in one bottle.

The semen analysis was fine—actually, perfect! Ahem! So off to the fertility expert in Albuquerque.

First, we drove to my office, since her period was late. Time for another pregnancy test—no luck. We drove the 120 miles to the doctor's office. He advised us to go right to in vitro fertilization, since Cathy was 35. Since this procedure was not covered by insurance, it would cost us $7,500, the equivalent of $20,000 today.

We drove home disappointed. Cathy's eyes welled up. I knew how much she wanted a child. By now I wanted to have a child with her, and felt inside that we would do it—go ahead with the in vitro procedure. Her pain was right on the surface, but my pain was because of her pain. So I said, "Let's go for it!"

The next day, she came into my office and urinated into a cup. Discouraged and sure the results would be negative again, she hurried off before I could run the test. Two minutes later, I saw the double blue line—she was pregnant! I still have the stick the test was run on.

I ran to see if she was in the parking lot. No go. I called her at home. The damn answering machine! "Cathy! Call me! Call me!"

Five minutes later I called her again. This time she picked up.

"You're pregnant!" I said.

"What!! No way. Are you kidding me?"

She cried. And so did I.

Dimitra, San Cristobal, New Mexico 1996

We have been together now for 24 years. What does it mean to love someone fully? For me, it is to know that she has my back, and I hers. I can say anything, and not be judged. That she still has that twinkle, that mystery, that brashness; she is the truth-teller of my soul. Yes, all that, and her beauty, too.

Bidding for Children

Adopting one child won't change the world,
but for that child the world will change.

-Unknown author

t's 2000. I'm in a hot, light-green room, getting ready
to appear on ABC's *Morning Show* with host Sally Jesse
Raphael. How did I land on this show?

The call came late one evening. "Dr. Schreiber,
we want your opinion on fashion shows as a way to
place waiting children."

The producers knew my opinion, for heaven's
sake. They'd read a piece I had written, speaking
against this practice. Imagine: Here is little Stephanie,
dressed in pink. Look how pretty she looks. She likes
soccer, Barbies, and horses. Wouldn't you love to give
Stephanie a home? Oh, and don't forget (though she
won't tell you): She has been raped by her Uncle Vincent
numerous times. But it's all right. Just give her a Barbie;
she'll probably survive.

You see the Sally Jesse Raphael show wanted
conflict. That's why they also booked a family who had
adopted a child from such a fashion runway show.

As for me, I felt passionately that the public
should know about the plight of waiting children and
the dedication and knowledge it takes to raise a child
who has been abused or neglected. At this point, I
was the co-founder and president of Child-Rite, New

Mexico's only private agency that dealt with special-needs children: children who had been physically or emotionally abused, minority children, children older than eight, or sibling groups. This was the "federal" definition, but the most special thing about these children was that they had no permanent home.

Children cannot be bought and sold. Money should not be an obstacle in becoming someone's son or daughter. That is why we never charged for our services. America's foster-care system is the training ground for the homeless, the street people, the psychiatric hospitals, and the jails and prisons throughout the United States.

Over its 20 years, Child-Rite placed 246 children who otherwise would have emancipated from foster care, with no anchor, no place to call home, no place for the holidays. When Child-Rite placed a child, we did so with honesty—and had the family commit on paper a hundred percent before exposing a child to more loss. We would always pitch the positive but never withhold information. The transaction was as pure as the children should have been.

However, it was also covert, this recruitment, so that the Stephanies never knew they were being rejected. What sickened me about these so-called fashion shows was partly the rejection: If the child was not chosen, off came the pretty party dress, returned to Macy's, and for you, Stephanie, it's back to the foster home. Back to a life of rejection. Perhaps as cruel was that the parents had not been prepared for the harsh reality that would follow.

I learned this the hard way. I, too, had once felt that love conquered all. But these children had been abused, raped, burned, unloved, moved, and shifted around like furniture. They were streetwise and knew how to smile at a potential parent. They knew how to hide their feelings and could perform well for a couple of months after being adopted. Then the bed wetting, the screams of terror, the stealing, the fury. They couldn't help it.

So when Sally Jesse Raphael's producer called and asked me to fly to New York and espouse my views on fashion shows displaying children for adoption, I jumped at the opportunity.

On the plane trip to New York, I wondered: Who thought this up? Fashion shows with orphans in the shopping malls of America showing off America's waiting children, where they are paraded up and down in borrowed clothing, as adults watching the show 'fall in love' and miraculously become insightful, special-needs parents.

Picking a child is not like picking a used car or clothing off the rack. It takes experience, education, and meticulously executed hard work. Heartstrings are not sufficient to make a competent parent for these traumatized children who have suffered unimaginable things. Sometimes, in fact, heartstrings hamper one's ability to act in the best interests of the child. Sentimentality often leads to failure. The worst happens: the family ruptures—because they are blinded by their emotions and not prepared for the havoc that follows placement—and the child goes back to foster care.

We haven't evolved much since the 1880s, when children were loaded on 'orphan trains' headed out West where they were to be 'chosen' to become a worker in families. Strength was needed to plow, haul water, herd cows, plant corn or wheat, or whatever. The 'weak-lings' who were not chosen were shipped back to their orphanages in New York or Boston or Philadelphia.

All of this had been going through my mind as I traveled toward my appearance on the TV program. After I arrived, they kept me backstage, isolated from my potential combatants, the parents who found their daughter in just such a show and lived happily ever after. Of course that child had been placed only three months ago. The family was still on their honeymoon high. What I would like to see, I thought to myself, is this family in three years.

I waited nervously as the makeup man applied his finishing touches. The commercial started, and Sally's assistant led me out onto the stage. I sat next to the host, but Sally never said hello or made eye contact. Only after she looked at her notes, did she turn to me: "You'll be on till the next commercial."

Turning to the audience, she said, "Welcome back folks."

I was usually a pretty good speaker about my passion, so TV sound bites fit me fine. "Children cannot be paraded," I said. "Show them on paper, don't view them publicly."

Sally Jesse seemed to be on my side. When the commercial came and I rose to leave, Sally asked me to stay for another segment. The parents of the fashion-show family were on deck. I smiled but they ignored the greeting. They told the story of how their 'perfect' family would never have existed without the fashion show. God had placed that child on that runway just for them.

I was speechless. While the Lungrin family spoke of their 'miracle' daughter, my mind drifted to Stephanie. I imagined her getting up that windy Saturday morning in March, putting on her borrowed dress, being picked up and driven to the Coronado Mall by a social worker. At the mall, she would carefully walk up and down the runway, turning and twirling, hoping that someone would notice. But no one did; most of the time no one did. Then Stephanie would be taken back to her foster home that night, and say good night to her third 'mother' that year.

When the Lungrin family finished their segment, Sally turned to me and asked, "Well, Doctor, what do you think of the Lungrin's story?"

I could only reply "It seems to have worked for them." When the next commercial came, Sally asked me to leave.

Father and Doctor

I n medicine we strive to keep order, follow protocols. Yet we must constantly deal with messes: hemorrhages and holes that must be filled and repaired before we can return to our protocols. We have to be flexible, ready at all times to pivot on a dime. There are inspirational leaps, where the protocol is the backbone, but it's our own intuitional insights and actions that spark the fire that changes the course for the patient.

Then there is being a father. Similar rules apply. I had adopted YoRi when she was nine months old, the youngest child we had adopted. As a parent, we always see the infant, child, toddler, inside the adult. I remember YoRi and how she came off the plane from South Korea. The first time I held her in my arms, light as a feather. How she slept on a blanket on the floor of our room at Writer's Manor Hotel in Denver with her little tushy in the air.

And now here she was, 27 years later, in Operating Room B giving birth, and hemorrhaging—her blood was not clotting. The surgeon's sutures only created more tears, so pressure had to be applied on the wound to stop the bleeding. I feared I was watching the death of my daughter, not the birth of my granddaughter. YoRi had a complication of pregnancy, her placenta separated prematurely from the uterine wall. This led to disseminated intravascular coagulation. Red blood cells and platelets fell to dangerous levels, and clotting factors were consumed by mini clots throughout her body, leaving her without the ability to stop bleeding. Holy Cross Hospital, being a small and isolated facility in Northern New Mexico, did not have platelets, so the platelets would have to be transported by the New Mexico State Police from Santa Fe to Taos. The small amount of fresh frozen plasma that carries the clotting factors had to be thawed out in the hospital lab.

My son Lucas stood near my shoulder. Like me, he was a doctor—but also a brother to YoRi. We couldn't speak, fear lodged in our throats like stones. We looked at each other, silent, as YoRi continued to bleed. YoRi had seen too many operating rooms. Born with a cleft lip and palate, her face had been stretched and sewn, and put together by modern medicine—following protocols.

I thought over and over, "Will her life end here?" I was calm, which surprised me. Well, maybe focused is a better word. I thought if I just concentrated all my thoughts and feelings on her, I could keep her alive. If I just stayed by her, I could ward off the bleeding. I would be an instrument for saving her life. I could...

The operating room wasn't any different from the scores of others I had seen before. At chest level, separating YoRi's face from her body, was a metal rod draped with sterile blue paper. A white paper hat covered her hair, while the nurse anesthetist stood at her head, monitoring her vital signs. The surgeon operated from the right side of YoRi's body; next to her, the scrub nurse handed her instruments. On the left side stood the surgical assistant. A circulating nurse stood ready outside the sterile field. I stood six feet away on her left side, in scrubs next to Lucas, where we could see YoRi's face.

Soon, a tug of war developed inside me: father, doctor, father, doctor. I began shouting: "Thaw out the fresh frozen plasma, for heaven's sake."

Then the father whispered: "Don't let her die, God."

The doctor: "Get the platelets up from Santa Fe—now! She needs more red blood cells!"

The father: "Wipe the blood off her leg, please. Stroke her forehead; she loves that."

The pathologist and the medical lab technologists worked frantically to help save YoRi's life. Lucas and I watched until we could watch no more. First Lucas left. I stayed while the bleeding tapered. I thought about YoRi under stress, how her eyelids twitched; how she loved Kimchi; how she loved her sister Gabrielle following her around, and Michael carrying her on his hip the first summer we had adopted the two of them. When she was in a school play and forgot her line, she said aloud: "I'm sorry!" I wanted to grab her and say, "You'll be OK." I wanted to grab her off the operating table now and tell her: "YoRi, you will be OK."

YoRi stopped bleeding. The operating room assistant wheeled her to the ICU. Exhausted and exhilarated I went to see my granddaughter, who needed to be transferred to Albuquerque to a newborn intensive care unit. Liana was eight weeks early, her body pink, struggling to breathe.

It was February 14th, the wind so strong that the medical helicopter couldn't make it to Taos. So by ambulance we drove 12 miles to the Taos Airport, where a fixed-wing airplane waited to transport us. Once airborne I was bumped and thrown around like a beanbag as I held onto the shoulder harness that held me in my seat. Liana slept through the entire ride.

YoRi emerged from this trauma, touched and impressed by the lab team who'd helped save her life. She'd learned so much about blood clotting that seven years later she graduated with high honors from the University of New Mexico with a degree in Medical Laboratory Science. Today, she works in the hospital lab that helped save her life. And Liana frequently asks me: "Pop Pop, tell me about the airplane ride I took with you on the day I was born."

Liana and YoRi

Letter to Kevin

Today is May 23, 2010. I'm staring at Lobo Peak, covered still with the last remnants of snow. I'm sitting outside on the brick patio in a chair too small for me. The day after I got the news. You had died. Oh Kevin. My boy.

How do you go back over someone else's life? Can you find a pattern you missed when they were alive? It's been ten years since you left your home, my home, our home. Should I have run after you?

I saw your scars. Those almost perfect circles. It was a hot southern New Mexico day at the Holiday Inn in Clovis. The day we picked you and your sister Mary up to join our family. Eight-year-old Kevin—handsome, a crinkled smile, dimples.

You used to tell me you didn't remember those days of terror that gave you those scars. If only that were true. If I could have, I would have undone what had been done to you. The adults who hurt and abandoned you? I would go back and remake your story, so that when you arrived at our home, in the shelter of our home, you would have found no need to do harm to another—no impulse to do harm to yourself. But...

Kevin, was it your mother? One of her boyfriends? Your father? I can only imagine a predator, a human being with a need to hurt. Did the man linger while putting out his cigarette on your tender arm? Did you smell your flesh, burning? Did you scream?

Did your mother try to save you? Or did she merely drink and nod off? Oh, my son. I imagine it still. Clearly. An arm lifts the iron. Presses it, hot against your skin. Like a brand. The helplessness of you. The child you were. The child you never were. The adult you would never become. Now you are gone. So now this is it.

Should I have visited you? Flown to Indiana to see the apartment you lived in, the street you walked on, the daughter you created? Juliette. Kevin, did you take the pills and all the alcohol to dull your pain or did you really want out? I have question after question. None can be answered.

I remember the call from your wife, Karisenda. She said the EMTs had to tie your naked body to the stretcher. It took three men to restrain you. You, who were always so strong in body, so mild in temperament. But so troubling in your behavior. When the emergency room doctor told me they had to intubate you, I thought it was just to protect your airway from aspiration. I was in shock. Then, an hour later, at one in the morning, I got the final call: They couldn't resuscitate you. You had gone into ventricular fibrillation. I leapt out of bed, spun around, trying to understand, smashed my fist against the wall, trying to take this in, you in. Cathy sobbed. I phoned everyone—your brothers and sisters, your mother, my ex-wife, Carol. Mary, your protector and birth sister, who screamed, "Oh no, Pop! Oh no!"

The coroner ruled it a suicide. I don't think so.

They say that suicide, or what appears as suicide, is a hostile gesture. Not so much despair, but a way to remove oneself from others, to demand that they listen. What did I not hear when you were living with us?

Kevin

Memory feels sometimes like spinning slowly in air thick as molasses. I remember one summer night when I came home from working at the hospital. You were eating hotdogs and French fries. I remember you lifted your arm. And I saw. Those round circles. Fresh burns. Cigarettes. You did this to yourself. I caught my breath. Is this how he takes power over his own body? I wondered. And still I said nothing, Kevin. Did nothing. Denial is a strong thing, my son. I wanted to protect you from a truth you already knew.

I am circling around this. Here I am writing this letter. Is anything clearer today? Nothing. Not a goddamn thing.

Then later, as I continue trying to puzzle my way through your death, I remember reading the social service report, the 'pseudo' full disclosure of all children held hostage in the foster-care system. The social worker's log stated simply: "cigarette burns," "ironing scars"—as if they were wind, a snowstorm, some 'natural' occurrence.

If it had been my diagnosis, I would have written: Broken heart. Beaten body. Chances for full recovery: Zero. Prognosis: Dismal. Chances of giving out pain to others: Extremely likely.

But that's only hindsight. I miss you, Kevin. I'm sorry.

The question is not how to survive but how to thrive with passion, humor, and style.

—Maya Angelou

Parkinson's—the gift that keeps on taking.

—Michael J. Fox

A Slippery Slope

When I was diagnosed with Parkinson's, a friend of mine said: "At least you know what you have." Implying (I guess) that I know what will kill me, as opposed to not knowing. I told him: "We don't work on a quota system; I could still get cancer or heart disease."

As I age, and I accumulate other 'problems' that go along with aging, I become a more challenging 'patient.' My son Lucas has become my primary doctor. He wants it that way, and so do I. Still, is it fair that I burden my son? I ask myself that all the time. I worry about how stressful this must be for him. When I ask him about it, he says, "Pop, I'm fine."

Most people feel that doctors shouldn't treat members of their own families. But I have a special relationship with Lucas. I delivered him, at home. We've created a special bond. And I trust him more than any other physician.

With Parkinson's, I didn't say to myself: "Why me?" I don't believe in that. I've seen too many young people get horrible diseases, the fickleness of misery. A rabbi wrote a book titled, *When Bad Things Happen to Good People*. That's a great title for medical care. In fact for most of my practice, it seemed that 'bad' things did happen to mostly good people. Nobody *deserves* to suffer—well, maybe a few people. But being a doctor is not about making judgments on the quality of the patient, but on the quality of the pain.

With death it becomes dicier.

Like Jacob wrestling with the angel, I fight with myself when it comes to the issue of helping the dying versus my ethics: *Primum non nocere*—First, do no harm. To my patients or myself. I am a doctor. What that means precisely is that I doctor, without harm, and with the hope of relieving suffering. It means I cannot/will not 'kill' a patient—even if they ask me to do so. Yet, I will aggressively relieve suffering, even if that hastens death. It's a slippery slope.

We all die. We in this Western culture have tried to shield ourselves from confronting death—we spend more time planning a summer vacation than we do planning our end-of-life choices. It is not a 'fit' subject for conversation. Michael Mead once said, "We are a society that denies death. Therefore, we are walking toward death backwards. It is better to turn around."

The baby boomers, those who went to Vietnam and those of us who thought we could change the world, are now looking at our own deaths. How can this be denied? Most of those who survived Vietnam, or any of the more recent wars, or who have had a 'near death' experience, are not afraid of dying. The rest of us ask, am I afraid? How will I face it?

Now I see people of my generation who seem to think they can die the way they choose: on a Wednesday, or by planning their deaths so they don't have to suffer. I wish I were a bit more Buddhist about it, because it does seem that some suffering, even at the end of our lives, leads to growth, if only in the last weeks. At least that's what I've seen.

In the Affordable Care Act, there was a provision that doctors would be paid $200 to discuss end-of-life care with their patients, every five years. But because of the conservative shouts of 'death panels' this provision was erased. So, we'll pay huge sums for pacemakers, chemotherapy, defibrillators, and all the other mechanical means of sustaining life; but only a few dollars to the primary care doctor to discuss how we are going to die.

I'll tell you this: I want a peaceful death. I see myself surrounded by my large family, children, grandchildren, and my wife, Cathy, at home—before the great window, so I can look out on Lobo Peak. I am calm. I have no 'terminal agitation,' the kind of trembling hallucinatory state that sometimes affects those who are dying.

Yet I know that, regardless of any expectations, I don't know, can't know, what I'm going to be like, or do, or say, until I am inside the dying.

I tell my patients there's no 'correct' way to die. Yet still, I strive for a 'perfect' ending—for my patients and for myself.

My mother had what I'd call a peaceful death. A comic until the end, when I arrived in South Florida to be with her, she cried: "I thought I would die before you got here. And if I did I would have killed myself." She wasn't spiritual or religious at all. When I asked her if she was afraid of dying, she said: "No. I just enjoy living. But I am fearful of the 'mechanics' of dying. Will I gurgle, fill up with fluid, will I have pain?"

I told her I would take care of the mechanics. That was the least I could do. I acted both as doctor and son. I was proud of her. She was feisty to the end. When she was dying, she had myoclonus, a twitching of the muscles of her feet, caused by morphine. As a family, we were sure she was doing a final dance for us.

Most people want the kind of death I wish for myself. In fact, in a survey, 80 percent of those asked said they'd want to die at home; yet, 80 percent die in hospitals or nursing homes. Why?

Often it's because people panic, change their minds, and decide to fight until the end. Then they rush to the hospital and end up in the ER or the ICU. The ICU and emergency rooms are great places to go to save lives. For a heart attack, major trauma, infectious diseases— great; for dying, however, not so good. Hooked up to IV tubes and respirators, bright lights on all the time, and those beeping and buzzing sounds—burning up the soul.

There is a second reason. The institutionalization of dying: 25 percent of the Medicare budget is spent in the last year of a patient's life, 10 percent in the last month. Think about that.

Patients ask me to help them die. I take my advice from those who have thought deeply about suffering. Thomas Aquinas has already given us a doctrine to use: The Principle of Double Effect. He had four criteria:

1. The action itself must be morally good or at least indifferent.

2. The agent may not positively will the bad effect but may permit it.

3. The good effect must be produced by action, not the bad effect.

4. The good effect must be at least equal in importance to the bad effect.

For me, as long as the goal is to relieve suffering, death is an acceptable outcome. Therefore, I feel comfortable, if the patient does, in giving as much morphine and sedatives as needed to alleviate anguish, even if it hastens death, for death is not the goal.

I interned at University of New Mexico Medical Center on the internal medicine ward. One night in 1972, I returned to the room of a 75-year-old woman who had suffered a massive stroke. We had seen her earlier on our rounds. Her gray hair lay like strings around her head, her eyes sunken. She now existed in a vegetative state, with no hope of regaining any level of functioning. In those years, we kept people alive on IV fluids, prolonging not their life but their death, and in fact causing more suffering for the patient by flooding the lungs with fluids. The 'death rattle' is caused by these increased fluids common in hospital deaths.

Earlier that day, her daughter caught me in the hallway. "Can't you do something, Dr. Schreiber? Can't you end my mother's suffering?" The daughter was desperate. Her husband, standing there, also pushed for an ending. "She doesn't know us. There is no 'there' there."

Was I simply prolonging her death, and not her life? Yes. The family begged me to end the woman's travails. I refused their entreaties. At three in the morning, however, I awakened in the house staff quarters, stiff from the small cot on which I had to sleep. I walked quietly to the nurses' station, tiptoed past the bleached-blond nurse napping at her desk, head in her arms. I loaded a syringe with enough potassium to fell a horse then slipped into the old woman's room. I panicked. I stood by her body. No one to see—how easy it would be. But I couldn't. She died 12 hours later. But not by my hand.

―――――――――

I'm not so clear, though, about my own death or, in fact, about patients I know personally, or about some of the *real* slippery slopes of aiding the dying. For example, when I'm treating 'terminal agitation,' I know the end result is almost always death. So is it truly wrong to prescribe medication for the patient to take on their own schedule, when death is certain in the immediate future? If I offer a prescription for barbiturates, for the patient to take themselves, am I offering them a way to die by their own hand? Are they dying because I gave them the prescription or are they dying from their disease? Is the next step euthanasia?

As a general principle, I will not kill. But—and there are so many 'buts' that I have to go step by step, each patient being a whole universe of questions and answers. I must in the end be the judge of my own actions. As long as I do no harm.

Climbing

Occasionally in this collection of stories and vignettes, I've mentioned my love of climbing. I was adventurous when I was young, but in a different way. Never physically, unless you count riding a motorcycle, or my brief time in Little League, or running track and playing soccer in the ninth grade. When I settled into life in Northern New Mexico, the mountains, and peaks and trails—their sheer number, variety, and splendor—made hiking and climbing irresistible. I didn't scale 90-degree cliff walls or things like that. But I became a good hiker and an adequate climber. It's kept me young and fit, and I've traveled the world to confront a famous mountain's challenges. Of course, my adventures didn't prevent me from getting Parkinson's. But they've given me many moments of joy—and quite a number of scares.

Looking up the ice wall at 19,000 feet, I realized two things: my heart couldn't go any faster, and I couldn't go any slower.

In Nepal, at 20,000 feet, roped in to the lead Sherpa, holding on to the fixed ropes anchored into the mountain (the Sherpas climb the mountain twice: once to fix the ropes, and a second time to guide you up), I felt free, unencumbered by anything. There was nothing but the mountain, nothing but the next step. I was in the moment, breathing. My mind couldn't drift, in fact shouldn't drift. In Nepal, they have a saying: When you walk, walk; when you talk, talk; when you look, look.

Nepal, 2004

I first went to Nepal to trek, not to climb. Trekking is hiking; climbing in Nepal means putting on crampons in order to grip the glacier's ice and being able to handle ropes with a Jumar ascender, which slides up the rope. The Jumar has a brake, so if you slip, you don't tumble down the mountain. You don't need any special climbing skills—just aerobic conditioning, no fear of heights, and the ability to follow Sherpa directions.

My plan was to trek. But when I arrived at the glacier, everything changed. I decided I wanted to climb after all, to venture out into the vast unknown, and, smart me, I had brought along crampons, just in case. That night before my first climb, I was so ambivalent I couldn't sleep. I listened to small avalanches in the distance, the still of the night, and thought of my children. Yet I had to go. Why? Was I not fulfilled? Was it a Hemingway, pseudo-macho type of thing? A redemption for my brief stay at The Citadel?

Come morning, I put on my crampons and walked onto the white glacial sheet. The sky was almost too blue to believe. Clarity of sky—and of thinking. But oh, that wind. Howling, trying to chase me off the mountaintop. I climbed, tied to two Sherpas, jumping over small crevasses, feeling confident that they would fish me out if I fell in. After getting to 18,500 feet, I stopped, shy of the summit. I felt satisfied. There I was on the glacier, tied literally into the mountain, looking at Paldor Peak and north to Shishapangma, the only 8,000-meter peak in Tibet. I was eating kippers and felt what I thought was a bone in my mouth. *Aren't kippers boneless?* I reflexively spit it out—and watched my new molar crown go down the glacier, at the rate of about a dollar a foot.

That night on Paldor Mountain, we slept on the glacier. The Sherpas cautioned me not to go too far from the tent. They told me of how Babu Sherpa had fallen and died in a crevasse, allegedly while emptying his bowels. He had summited Everest more than any other human being. If falling into a crevasse could happen to him, it could surely happen to me. So, at two in the morning when nature called, I defecated outside the tent. I thought I would get rid of the evidence in the morning; but the evidence froze to the glacier sticking like a small boulder in a pristine plane. I tried to chip it away with my ice axe, no luck. The Sherpas walked by the tent in the morning and gleefully smiled, laughing, talking in their tongue and saying something I couldn't understand. But it ended with 'Larry.'

On the glacier you dream of a hot bath, of eating a steak. But when I got home to Taos, I dreamt only of the glacier—how beautiful it had been, how terrifying. After nights of dreaming this, I realized I needed a Himalayan summit, a reaching of a mountain's top. So, three years later, in 2004, I went to the Khumbu region—where Everest is—to climb Island Peak and Pokalde.

My five fellow climbers and I landed in a small fixed plane at the small town of Lukla, in Nepal, at 9,500 feet. The runway went uphill and everyone applauded when we landed, grateful to be alive. We then trekked to Namche Bazaar, the Sherpa capital. We reached this hillside gem at 11,000 feet on a Saturday, the day the Tibetans came to trade their wares with the Sherpas, who had the means to buy Tibetan goods: clothes, vests, jewelry. The Sherpas were considered wealthy from the money they made guiding Westerners up the mountains.

From Namche, we hiked to Syangboche, with its unpaved landing strip at 13,000 feet and where the Japanese had once built a hotel. Rooms at the hotel came outfitted with oxygen connections, just like in a hospital, because the tourists who came in on airplanes hadn't acclimated like the hikers; without oxygen they would have developed acute mountain sickness. The hotel didn't work out, however. It had closed, leaving only a restaurant. We didn't stop to eat, though. From Syangboche we hiked to Tengboche, where we received a blessing from the monks. They placed catas, prayer shawls, around our necks. We drank tea. Then it was off to a nunnery, where I meditated for two hours with elderly nuns who spoke no English. But I felt more at home there than with some of the climbers I met.

Our party slept at tea houses. The rooms were like cardboard: no heat, except in the dining room, where a metal woodburning stove was kept lit by the Sherpas. We would stay in the dining room until the sun went down, then retreat to the dingy rooms, where we would listen to other climbers cough. Coughing was constant from the dryness and the altitude. It was called the Khumbu cough.

We continued to the base camp for Island Peak. Now we were at 16,800 feet. Several climbers had been killed at the base camp a few years earlier by an avalanche. I hadn't wanted to tell Cathy about this before leaving for Nepal, but one night I had taken an Ambien to go to sleep. This sleeping pill sometimes acts like truth serum. Unbeknownst to me, I had woken Cathy in the middle of the night and told her the truth. Then I went back to sleep. The next morning, Cathy sarcastically said, "So tell me about base camp, and the avalanches!" I felt like I'd let out a dark secret and that Cathy now shared my fears. But Cathy said, "It's better to know, Larry."

At high camp, at 18,700 feet, you don't sleep well. You have interrupted sleep, partly because of altitude— you toss and turn; your gasping for breath wakes you up—and partly because of anxiety, knowing what you are going to do. At high camp, I took Diamox, a drug that lessens the danger of altitude sickness. It makes you breathe harder, so your oxygen stays up and your carbon dioxide goes down. It also acts like a diuretic, causing you to urinate more at night. You use a pee bottle to avoid going out in the freezing cold. One time, groping for the bottle, I knocked it over. "Oh damn, not now," I said to myself. But the urine from two hours earlier had frozen—one advantage of high-altitude mountaineering.

The climb started at three in the morning by the full moon. At high camp there were other climbers—mostly young, about my children's age. They said they were going to leave about five o'clock. I decided to leave at three. I did not want to have other climbers behind me on the ice wall. I felt enough pressure to climb without some young kid going, "Get up old man." We all had headlamps, but after acclimating to the darkness, we didn't need them. The full moon illuminated the ice, turning the world blue. On the glacier with me was John Hutchinson, the pharmacist from Holy Cross Hospital. I had asked him one day at the hospital if he'd like to go to Nepal, remembering how he'd once told me of his dreams of being on a glacier. On the glacier, he became ebullient, like a little boy. He shouted, "I am on the glacier, I am on the glacier! I can't believe it!"

Once I was on the ice wall, counting my pulse, I wasn't sure I could make it. I went so slowly that it was more like creeping than climbing. Finally, at 6:30 a.m., I made it to the ridge, and got to see the other side. Once on the ridge, I knew I could make it to the summit. The summit ridge was narrow. If I fell off to the left, I would end up in Tibet; to the right, Nepal.

At 8 a.m., we made it to the summit. It was empty. I looked south at Ama Dablam, the most beautiful mountain in the world. To the north the ice walls of Nuptse and Lhotse, both peaks hiding Everest. It literally, and figuratively, took my breath away. I thought I could stay there forever. I realized why they called it Island Peak. It floated in a sea of ice.

The Other Side

From the east window of my living room, I can see Lobo Peak.

My home is in a valley, in San Cristobal, New Mexico. I am surrounded by mountains. I know them all: Pueblo Peak, El Salto, Lobo; to the west, San Antonio and Ute; southwest, Picuris Peak, Truchas and Jemez. Sometimes, up in the mountains, I can just about make out Georgia O'Keefe's Pedernal 50 or 60 miles away to the west, the mountain O'Keefe painted so many times that God finally gave it to her.[1]

Names are important and at times seem to have magical power. Naming anything brings it closer, as if by naming it you've discovered its secret. Like naming a disease. Do you then become the disease? Are you still the same person, but in a new geography? As a doctor, I'm always looking for the name—the proper incantation. Could it be idiopathic Parkinson's? Or, Parkinson's-like symptoms, caused by a stroke or head trauma? It's my job to name it.

[1] Lesley Poling-Kempes, *Valley of Shining Stone: The Story of Abiquiu* (Tucson, AZ: The University of Arizona Press, 1997), p. 191. According to Poling-Kempes, "Cerro Pedernal was soon a frequent and familiar motif in O'Keeffe's work. From Ghost Ranch, Pedernal seems to be positioned so as to be quietly observing whatever and whomever moves on the desert between the great cliffs and the mountain. The longer one lives out on the Piedra Lumbre, the deeper one senses a shared intimacy, shared history, with the sacred cerro. 'It's my private mountain,' O'Keeffe said of the blue mountain. 'It belongs to me. God told me if I painted it enough, I could have it.'"

There's something in a name that pulls me to it, as when the neurologist confirmed the name of what I knew but rationalized away for years: Parkinson's.

I love my home in San Cristobal. What I see through my east window is the mountain range that I've climbed over and over, naming the peaks as I ascend, like a chant. The mountains are as familiar to me as the names of my children; they are old, dear friends.

I always think of mountains as female. I don't know why. They are to me welcoming, nurturing, unpredictable. We seem at first to cling to their skirts, climbing on up to their shoulders from where we see the world in a new way. I have a favorite trail: Gavilan. There's no peak, just a ridge, where, when I reach it I can see the other side.

Seeing the other side is one of those 'oh' moments. You've climbed a mountain with which you are familiar; your world becomes magnified. You gain a whole new perspective. It's a gift. But you can't see the other side unless you reach the ridge, then it is like suddenly finding another room in your home. And every season there is newness, and every hour the light changes.

Why do things seem so clear there yet so murky down below? I find clarity in the mountains, but density in my physical being. I know there must be another side to this life, but I can't believe in it yet. When I'm in the mountains I feel as if I know an answer to a question that has no words.

On the Gavilan ridge, the mountains change their colors: the light is gold at mid-day. In the meadow below the ridge, where aspens shiver, the greens are bright and silver, or tinted with a plum color...The sky behind the trees changes from a deep sea blue to a light blue, so pale that it is, almost white. All colors here are subtle, you must really look.

On some days the clouds come upon you quickly, warning you to leave. You see what we call 'walking rain' a vertical dark smudge in the sky, moving ominously toward you. On any ridge, lightning comes swiftly, sometimes only one or two seconds separate from the thunder. You feel the hair on your neck rise, and quickly you begin your journey down. She has shown her other side.

On Gavilan, you are surrounded by the other peaks in the Sangre de Cristo Range: Wheeler, Simpson, Walter, Kachina and Lake Fork. Wheeler Peak is the highest in New Mexico, at 13,161 feet. People who love mountains, love to name the height of them. No matter how doubtful I am when I set out, when I climb it's as if I've found my church.

Parkinson's affects my balance and makes my legs heavier, so I have to work harder physically to accomplish what once came naturally. I must consciously concentrate on lifting one leg at a time, which makes it seem like I'm climbing even when I'm on level ground. Three years ago, having already been diagnosed for several years, I realized that I could no longer make the technically difficult climbs. I could no longer be on ropes or hopping over crevasses. Still I longed for one of the great mountains. I picked Kilimanjaro, because it was not a technical climb; you don't need ropes, or crampons, or an ice ax.

When climbing uphill and pushing your body, you focus only on the breath, and sometimes when it's steep, like on Kilimanjaro, I could take only 20 steps, lean over my walking stick, breathe, listen to my heart. But it is this very physical exhaustion that is so exhilarating— even the suffering.

I went to Kilimanjaro in 2011. I took the photo of my son Kevin with me. He had died a year before, and I had buried his ashes on the north ridge, just above our home in San Cristobal. A spot I'm drawn to every day. To remember. My son. What could be more fitting than leaving his photo, this beautiful and tragic African-American boy, atop the highest point in Africa? Perhaps that was my real goal. To reach a kind of resolution, a freedom, or *uhuru.*

What will my freedom be? Bradykinesia, tremor, freezing gait—can I surmount these names? Are they simply powerless, empty labels? Will I get to the other side? Is there an *uhuru* point for me, metaphysically? Will I see another Mount Meru, or just darkness? When on Kilimanjaro on the ridge en route to the summit, there, spread before me, was Tanzania's Mount Meru, the vast gold plains of Africa, the sun rising on one side and the full moon setting on the other.

Kilimanjaro, 2011

In memory

April 14, 1947 — January 18, 2016

On January 12, 2016 Larry suffered a hemorrhagic stroke.
He remained alert, viewed the CT images of his brain, then
gently and courageously communicated to his wife, Cathy, and
his children that he wanted to be home to look out the large
picture window at Lobo Peak. On January 18, 2016 Larry died
peacefully surrounded by his family.

Biography

Larry Schreiber, M.D., lived in northern New Mexico and practiced medicine there for 43 years. He was the proud father of 14 children, ten of them adopted from around the world. He was married to poet, Catherine Strisik. For 20 years he served as medical director of Mountain Home Hospice of Taos. In 1980, Dr. Schreiber was a medical team leader for the international committee of the Red Cross on the Thai-Cambodian border. He was the co-founder of Child-Rite which operated for 20 years and placed 240 special needs children in New Mexico homes at no cost to the families. Dr. Schreiber spent the last three years of his life writing *A Life Well Worn*, a collection of autobiographical stories about children growing up (and down), his experiences in the Indian Health Services, memories of working in a war zone, and thoughts of caring for the dying in a rural community. He passed away in January of 2016, shortly after completing this book.

Made in the USA
Las Vegas, NV
07 October 2021